Nigel Bishop is head teacher at St[illegible] Grimsby, North East Lincolnshire [illegible] years, during which time he has taught children aged 4–11 in a wide range of schools in and around Grimsby and Cleethorpes, trying to share with them his passion for experiential learning. Nigel is also a Methodist Lay Preacher and has used his communication skills in all-age worship as well as numerous school assemblies. In his first book, *Stories for Interactive Assemblies*, Nigel recorded a series of stories that he had used orally to make the parables of Jesus more accessible to a young audience. In his latest book he draws on his early working life in agriculture, as well as two residential visits made to a farm in Gloucestershire with children from one of his previous schools. Nigel lives in Grimsby with his wife Jackie and their dog Tilly.

Barnabas in Schools

Barnabas in Schools® is a registered word mark and the logo is a registered device mark of The Bible Reading Fellowship.

Text copyright © Nigel Bishop 2012
The author asserts the moral right
to be identified as the author of this work

Published by
The Bible Reading Fellowship
15 The Chambers, Vineyard
Abingdon OX14 3FE
United Kingdom
Tel: +44 (0)1865 319700
Email: enquiries@brf.org.uk
Website: www.brf.org.uk
BRF is a Registered Charity

ISBN 978 1 84101 837 9

First published 2012
10 9 8 7 6 5 4 3 2 1 0
All rights reserved

The paper used in the production of this publication was supplied by mills that source their raw materials from sustainably managed forests. Soy-based inks were used in its printing and the laminate film is biodegradable.

A catalogue record for this book is available from the British Library

Printed in Singapore by Craft Print International Ltd

More Stories

FOR INTERACTIVE ASSEMBLIES

20 story-based assemblies to get children talking

NIGEL BISHOP

*With gratitude to all the colleagues and pupils
from whom I have learnt so much over the years.*

ACKNOWLEDGMENTS

I am indebted to my editor, Sue Doggett, whose encouragement and creative input have played such a crucial part in bringing my ideas to reality. I am also indebted to everyone at Farms for City Children, the marvellous organisation that introduced me to the benefits of taking town children for residential visits to a farm. As ever, I could have written nothing without the constant support and belief of my wonderful wife, Jackie.

Contents

Foreword 7

Introduction 8

1 I can't wait 11

2 You don't get out of it that easily 17

3 Follow the rules and you'll be fine 24

4 Sometimes it's good to give something up 31

5 Next time, think about it first, please 37

6 Pass the salt, please, mate 44

7 Never be afraid to say you don't know 51

8 Sorry, but it was me 57

9 Life's too short to hold grudges 64

10 It's just something someone gave me 71

11 I try to be helpful 77

12 You never see anything like this at home 84

13 I can't believe how quick you've been 90

14 I haven't felt this good in ages 96

15 I thought you'd nicked it 102

16 It can be amazing, too 108

17 It was nothing 114

18 I'm good, thanks 120

19 I've got everything I want in here 126

20 A lot can change in a week 132

Index of curriculum and biblical links 138

Foreword

Nigel Bishop has a true storyteller's gift for the lively detail, the telling phrase and the twist in the tail. His vision of school assembly is that it will make you think: you might ask a question of yourself and challenge your values. By bringing his gifts as a storyteller together with his vision in these 20 stories, he has created a tool for good assembly that pupils and teachers will love.

Here you will find 20 linked but independent stories bundled together with a narrative about a week's school trip to a farm. Each story sparkles with well-thought-out characters and plot developments that make the familiar life of a school into a series of provocative jumping-off points for reflection: what kind of person do I want to be? Why do I sometimes disappoint myself? What's the best thing to do when things go wrong?

Well-crafted thinking points emerge from each part of the narrative. Themes of rules or friendship, forgiveness or bravery, honesty or perseverance get some attention in a natural way. The biblical quotations that have been in Nigel's mind are clear and are listed at the end—but never feel like something being pushed down your throat.

Busy teachers often struggle to make assembly work well. This book gives you something ready to use but also something to bring a sense of occasion to the whole school gathering. Your school may not be able to take a class of children on a week's trip to a Derbyshire farm, but going there through these stories is possible for every reader.

If you want your assemblies to be alive, creative, spiritually provocative and interesting, read on.

Lat Blaylock, RE adviser with RE Today

Introduction

In my first book, *Stories for Interactive Assemblies*, I used 15 of the parables of Jesus as the basis for a set of unrelated short stories for use in assemblies or the classroom. When Jesus told his parables, he took the everyday world of his listeners and used it as the backdrop for easily recognisable characters and events that would carry his message. The Gospels seldom record any explanation of the stories, implying that Jesus understood the power of a narrative to get past people's guard and influence the views and attitudes of his audience. Generally speaking, the parables are not obviously 'religious' stories at all, although we tend to think of them in that way, so frequently have we encountered them as part of the biblical text. As a preacher and teacher, I wanted to find a way to communicate the messages that I believe Jesus intended through a medium familiar to primary-aged children, so I reset the parables in the primary school and its surroundings.

I had always anticipated the possibility of a second book, so I turned my thoughts to another project that had been in the back of my mind for a while. While I was a deputy head teacher in one of our Grimsby primary schools, I was instrumental in setting up an annual visit to Wick Court Farm in Gloucestershire, run by a fabulous charity called Farms for City Children. We shared the venture with two other schools and took a group of 30 children in total. I was fortunate enough to go on two of these week-long residential visits before moving to a headship in Lincolnshire. Some ten years later, the visit is still very much part of the three schools' calendars, and, I'm sure, is still much appreciated by staff and pupils alike.

During my early working life I worked on farms in Derbyshire and Lincolnshire before moving into teaching via youth work and pastoral support in the Methodist Church. Having seen at first hand the transforming power of farm visits for town children, and having a working knowledge of many aspects of farming (although much has changed in the 25 years since I pulled on mucky wellies in earnest), I decided to write a new set of parables, linked by the structure of a residential trip and developing a single set of characters, including 20 children, each of whom would feature in one of the chapters. The parables are intended to illustrate central Judeo-Christian truths, with rather more emphasis on the gospel dimension where there is a clash between the Old Testament perspective and the ideas of Jesus. The abiding tone of most of the stories is intended to be the transforming power of unconditional love, an aspect of Jesus' ministry that so many of us try to emulate daily in our working lives.

The idea evolved into the book that you have in your hands now. Each of the 20 chapters is a stand-alone story, although the series fits together into a chronological account if you would like to use it in that way. I decided not to add follow-up activities this time, concentrating more on the narrative possibilities, although I have included some aspects of my first book's structure. There is a brief indication as to what each story is about, a small number of warm-up questions to precede each story (intended to encourage the listeners to be more receptive) and a short prayer in case you are using the story in a worship setting. I have also added five follow-up questions for each chapter so that you can extend the children's understanding if you want to. I have consciously aimed this book at Key Stage Two pupils, although I have found that Year Two children can understand much of the material that I've shared with them, as long as I tell the stories rather than reading them. I usually find storytelling more engaging and therefore more effective than reading, especially to a mass audience like a group of children in assembly, and I would encourage you to read the story first before retelling it in your own words, based on your own recall.

It might also help to change some of the names to suit your own circumstances.

In this book I was also keen that children should be able to read the stories for themselves, and that teachers should be able to use the material almost as a class-reader. I admit that I haven't tried the stories in that context, not having a class of my own at the moment, but I see no reason why it wouldn't work, given a class with sufficient powers of attention and understanding.

I hope you find the book useful and that the children with whom you share it discover some of the challenging and exciting truths of a faith that has guided me, with varying degrees of success, throughout my life. You will note that I haven't generally related the stories overtly to religious ideas or activities. I leave you to make whatever links you wish to your own experience or understanding of faith, and the index of curriculum and biblical links should give you some ideas in that respect. The need to have a professional, non-proselytising approach as a head teacher has caused me to be deliberately reticent in this respect. However, as I have indicated above, using Jesus as my model leads me to believe that non-religious stories have great power to convey religious ideas to considerable effect.

1

I can't wait

> ### WHAT'S IT ABOUT?
>
> When Mrs Denly, the head teacher of Winding Way Primary School, tells the children about a residential trip to a farm in Derbyshire, how will Kaci respond?

The children filed quietly into the hall, filling the large, airy space from two different doors—one for infants and the other for juniors. The gentle sounds of music drifted out of the two speakers mounted high on the front wall and, for any of the children who were curious, a small printed notice announced, 'This week's music is "Spring" by Antonio Vivaldi, 1723'. When everyone was settled and the music had been turned off, the head teacher, Mrs Denly, led the school in its normal sing-song greeting of 'Good morning, everybody.' Once this had been completed, she introduced the theme for the morning's assembly.

'I've got something to tell you all,' she said, her voice crackling with the excitement of someone about to share a secret. 'I've managed to set up a link with a farm. It's a long way away, in a county called Derbyshire.'

Mrs Denly turned on her laptop and asked Jade-Marie from Year Six to push the keys to show a presentation on the big screen. There were some photographs of farm animals—a huge, grinning pig with black spots on a hairy pink skin, some very woolly sheep with curly horns, and a brown and white cow with large, liquid eyes. Then there was a tractor, bright and shiny red, pulling a trailer full of bales of straw, followed by a green and yellow combine harvester munching its way through a field of golden barley. Finally came a series of pictures of a brick-built farm house surrounded by a low stone wall, with a large dining-room, a steep staircase leading to the two upper floors of cosy-looking dormitories, each with six bunks in them, and a tiny classroom perched at the very top. This last room was full of sunshine angling in through the large dormer windows that gazed unblinkingly down from the grey slate roof on to the farmyard below and the steep, rocky slopes beyond.

'I'm delighted to be able to tell you that we are taking 20 children to the farm at the end of September,' explained Mrs Denly, beaming with pleasure. Everyone knew that she had grown up on a farm because she often talked about it in assemblies, so that explained why she would be going too. 'We'll be there for nearly a week, from Monday afternoon to Friday morning, and the visit will be open to Years Five and Six.'

There was a gasp of excitement from the oldest juniors, at the same time as a soft groan from some of the younger children in the hall. Mrs Denly responded immediately by explaining that if the trip was a success, it would definitely be repeated in two years' time.

'The letters will be given out at home time and the office will text your parents to let them know about it,' continued Mrs Denly, showing a letter to the children as she spoke, and pointing out the form that their parents had to fill in if they wanted their child to go. 'You will need to bring a £5 deposit in to me first thing in the morning,' she explained. 'It'll be first-come first-served, so you'll have to get your skates on.' This last comment was greeted by excited whispering from the Year Fives and Sixes at the back of the hall.

Kaci sat quietly on the back row, feeling her heart thumping inside her chest. It was always the same when she thought about being away from home. She'd tried so many times before—sleepovers, Brownie camp, going to stay with her nanna just 20 miles away, but on each occasion she'd had to give in and come home again. For Brownie camp during the Easter holidays, she'd got as far as the coach, with her rucksack on her back and her suitcase in her sweaty hand, only to have to walk home with Mum at the last minute, blinking away the tears of shame and regret. But this farm trip would be perfect. She loved animals—always had. She thought of Megan the dog, Midnight the cat and her two rabbits, Ant and Dec, at home. Pets had always been a part of her life, and the thought of being on a farm with so many new friends to stroke and feed and even clean out was almost more than she could imagine. The trouble was, as much as she longed to go, she just couldn't picture herself bringing the form and the deposit back and giving them to Mrs Denly. Well, perhaps she could, but then getting on the coach and waving goodbye to her mum was bound to be a challenge too far. 'I suppose there's no harm in taking the letter home,' she decided.

Martin, on the other hand, was supremely confident about staying away from home. Only three weeks before, he'd gone to a football tournament with the under-10s team—he played in goal—and he'd had a great time. They'd slept in tents, two in each one, and the smell of canvas and wet grass seemed still to be in his nostrils when he let the memory replay through his mind. He remembered his mum saying that she couldn't wait for the next time he went away—although he wasn't sure that this was a good thing. 'The longer he's out of the house, the better,' she'd said to his stepdad, laughing heartily, but perhaps she wasn't altogether as cheerful about it as she had seemed. The tractors and other machinery had caught Martin's eye the most as he watched Mrs Denly's presentation. He resolved to take the letter straight home that night so that he could be one of the first people to get a completed form in.

Kaci's mum was unloading the dishwasher when Kaci opened the kitchen door and stepped on to the doormat just inside.

'What's all this about a farm trip?' asked Mum, pointing to her mobile phone, which was lying on the worktop. 'The school says you should have a letter for me.' Kaci nodded, reaching into her book bag as she did so. Her fingers closed uncertainly on the paper inside, but she pulled it out with the most convincing smile she could manage and handed it to her mum, who read its contents quietly and carefully.

'Is there any point sending the form back, do you think?' wondered Mum almost to herself when she'd finished reading, although she did look encouragingly at her daughter as she spoke. Kaci let the question hang in the air for a few moments, listening to her heart beating and wondering whether Mum could hear it too on the other side of the kitchen.

'I really want to go this time,' she said finally, although she wished immediately that her voice had sounded more convincing.

The next morning, Martin slammed the front door behind him and dashed up the path, slinging his black rucksack on to his back as he did so. He'd grabbed the trip form as he'd passed the shelf in the hall, and he patted his trouser pocket to check that the plastic bag with five pound coins inside was safely there with it. Hardly anyone was in the playground when he arrived, and he waited as patiently as he could for the Breakfast Club door to open. Mrs Denly herself turned the lock and welcomed the chattering group of children into the dining-room.

'You're the first one,' she said to Martin as he delved under his hanky for the folded paper and the heavy bag of coins. Having dropped them both into Mrs Denly's outstretched hand, he dumped his coat and bag on to the pile against the wall and hurried across to the hatch to get his usual bowl of Sugar Puffs.

When Mum pulled into the drop-off zone outside the school gate, Kaci was relieved to see through the passenger side window that her friend Lara was waiting for her by the railings.

'See you tonight, Mum,' she murmured, noticing the encouraging look that her mum shone at her. As she pushed the heavy car door to with a satisfying clunk, Kaci knew that she could hand the form and the £5 note to Mrs Denly quite easily, but she was far from sure that she would be able to see it through and actually go on the trip in September. So what was the point?

'Are you coming?' asked Lara, sensing her friend's uncertainty as they walked together towards the Junior entrance.

'I don't think I'll bother after all,' Kaci said, trying to sound decisive.

'This time you'll do it, I just know,' replied Lara, putting her arm round Kaci's shoulders and squeezing fiercely. 'Remember our swimming lesson yesterday. What did the teacher say?'

Kaci thought back to the previous day's trip to the local pool with the rest of their class, and the words of the young woman who'd finally persuaded her to try without any floats at all.

'Go for it even if you feel frightened.' She recited the phrase to herself now as she walked up to Mrs Denly on the playground, and, for the first time since she'd seen the pictures of the farm, she really believed that this time she would be on that coach.

'Well done, Lara and Kaci. That leaves just one place to fill,' said Mrs Denly, beaming with pleasure. 'How do you feel about going, Kaci?' she added as an afterthought.

Kaci stuck out her chin. 'I can't wait!' came the determined reply.

MENTAL SWITCH-ON

How do you feel about the thought of staying away from home? What's the furthest away that you've ever travelled from home? When you've decided to do something, do you ever have second thoughts?

SO WHAT?

- How does it feel when you're about to tell people something that they don't know?
- What do you think the children might have been whispering to each other when Mrs Denly said that places would be 'first-come first-served'?
- How do you think Martin felt about what his mum said to his stepdad?
- What would you most like to do if you could? What's stopping you?
- Have you ever been in a situation where the swimming teacher's advice would have been helpful?

PRAYER

Help us to challenge ourselves and support each other,
so that together we can grow.
Amen

2

You don't get out of it that easily

> **WHAT'S IT ABOUT?**
>
> Will Ashley's behaviour stop him going on the trip?

Ashley pressed the button at the main entrance and walked into the reception area when the electronic door release clicked. He slapped the brown envelope on to the wooden countertop and looked up into the jolly face of Mrs Shearer, the administrator.

'Take your hood off inside, please,' she said, gently but in a way that Ashley didn't feel he could argue with. 'What's this, then?' she continued.

'It's my form for the farm,' Ashley explained bluntly. 'My mum says I've got to go so she can have some peace and quiet for a week.'

'I'm sure she doesn't really mean that,' said Mrs Shearer with a forced chuckle—she didn't sound convinced. Everyone at Winding Way Primary School knew Ashley only too well. There would be many other people who would be pleased to see the back of him for a week. It would just be a shame for the other people going on the trip, thought Mrs Shearer.

Ashley waited, fidgeting, while the administrator tore open the envelope and pulled out the form. She checked the signature carefully and pushed her hand into the envelope, exploring its dark interior carefully with a thoughtful look on her face. Eventually she asked, 'Where's the money, please, Ashley?'

'Oh, my mum says, can she pay next week?' he answered. Before Mrs Shearer could reply, Ashley was gone, heading for the door into the main building with his head down and his lunch bag swinging jauntily from his wrist. Mrs Shearer pressed the release button beside her computer to let him through. It was too early in the day for an argument, especially with Ashley. She would let Mrs Denly, the head teacher, deal with it later.

As it happened, it wasn't long before Mrs Denly had the chance to talk to Ashley. When she came out of the staff room at the end of morning break, she found him loitering outside her office with the usual look on his face, a look she'd come to know only too well over the two years since he'd come to the school. Switching her mind into 'super-positive mode', she walked briskly up to him and opened her office door.

'Why don't you come in and tell me all about it,' she suggested, quietly but firmly.

Ashley followed her into the room and stood by the desk, fiddling with the paperclips that were always to be found in a small glass container next to the photograph of Mrs Denly's two children. Ashley was very familiar with the photograph of a boy and a girl, both smiling out of the light wooden frame. He thought again of his own family. Four brothers and sisters. Almost too much competition for his mum's attention most of the time, he thought—and too much responsibility when she wasn't coping.

Ashley's thoughts were dragged back to the head teacher's

office by Mrs Denly's voice asking the usual question: 'What seems to be the problem this time?'

'They were winding me up,' he replied by way of an introduction. The full story was then dragged out of him, slowly and painstakingly, with notes jotted down on a piece of paper so that Mrs Denly could see the other children involved and check his version of events. Of course, there was also the inevitable question about what he could, and should, have done differently. It was easy for Mrs Denly. She hadn't been there, had she, with their faces all staring at her and their whispering echoing in her ears.

'I know things aren't easy for you sometimes,' she finished as usual, 'but it's really no excuse for punching people.' Ashley knew he'd have to stay in for two break times and lunch times to write out the school's key values, but in many ways that would be easier than going out on to the playground. Unfortunately, he'd miss his football, too, of course—the time when he felt most alive—but that couldn't be helped. Ashley was about to ask whether he should go back to class when Mrs Denly suddenly changed gear.

'I see you've brought your form back for the farm,' she said. 'Would you like me to have a word with your mum about the money when she picks you up tonight?'

'You said we had to bring in five pounds this morning,' Ashley pointed out, sulkily.

'I know, but I might be able to make an exception in your case. I know your mum's had a lot to deal with lately, and we do have some money in our Opportunity Fund. Would you really like to go?'

Ashley thought for a moment—thought about being away from home for a week, away from school, away from the playground...

'I suppose so,' he mumbled before heading out of the room.

'I'll come and check that you've settled into Maths in five minutes.' Mrs Denly's words reached him in the corridor. He could feel her disappointment seeping into him like a liquid, but as usual it made him feel good in a way that he couldn't explain. Not to anyone.

After he had eaten his lunch, Ashley kept his head down and tried to get back on to the playground through the dining-room door. Why should he miss his football? OK, so he always fell out with someone over a bad tackle or a goal that shouldn't have been allowed, but there was nothing like the feeling of putting your foot through the ball so hard that the keeper didn't stand a chance. However, the vigilant Mrs Soames, senior lunch-time supervisor, moved her ample body into his path, her black plastic-covered clipboard acting as a first line of defence.

'I see you've got lines, Ashley. Best get them done without a fuss.' Ashley changed direction, back towards the lines room along the corridor, and noticed Mrs Denly busily putting up a display about the farm. She had printed off some photos from the website and was stapling them up on a background of rich green paper, along with some printed questions and answers to let the children know what awaited them if they went. An idea formed instantly in Ashley's mind. He knew exactly what he was going to do. He'd show Mrs Denly. He'd show them all.

When Ashley finished his lines, there were only five minutes until the afternoon session, so Mr Piper, the deputy head teacher, let him out early—'for good behaviour', as he always put it.

'Have a quick run round the playground, Ashley,' he suggested, 'but make sure you keep out of trouble.'

Mr Piper then hurried off to the staff room, where there would just be time for him to grab a few sips from the tepid coffee he'd made earlier, before going to collect his class. As soon as Mr Piper had gone through the staff room door, Ashley returned from the corridor porch where he had been waiting. He pulled the photographs, one at a time, from the display board, savouring each tiny tearing sound that the staples made on the paper as he did so. Then it was the turn of the written questions and answers, which he rolled into a series of tight balls with his right fist as he tore each piece away from the backing paper. When he had finished, the corridor floor was strewn randomly with a mixture of creased oblongs and crumpled mounds of paper. His heart hammering in his chest, Ashley ran to the end of the corridor, bursting out into the harsh brightness and the shrieking babble of the last two minutes of lunch break.

Mrs Denly was sitting very still behind her desk when Ashley came into her room. His mum was sitting on a chair in the corner, her eyes studying the carpet. The buggy was outside in the corridor, and she had his baby sister Kirsten wriggling on her knee. He thought about tickling Kirsten but thought better of it when his mum looked up at him.

'Sit down, please, Ashley,' instructed Mrs Denly. 'I've asked your mum to join us because I want to sort out about the farm. I think you want to go, and I think it will do you a lot of good to go, and I want you to know that what you did to my display won't change that.'

Kirsten gurgled noisily, the sound invading the silence that had filled the room for just a few seconds.

'I've spoken to your mum about paying for the trip and we've come to an arrangement,' continued Mrs Denly. 'I think that you can keep your behaviour right until we go, and while we're there, of course. Because even though you don't always believe in yourself, I want you to know that I do, and I think your mum does too. Now get yourself home and let's have a much better day tomorrow, please.'

Mum stood up wearily, with a glance at Ashley that showed she agreed with the head teacher, at least for now. As they were going through the door to collect the buggy and Ashley's other two brothers, who'd been brought down by their own teachers at home time, Mrs Denly spoke again, leaning against her desk as she did so.

'Sometimes it's only possible to turn your own life round because someone else, maybe just one person, is sure that you can do it. Don't miss this chance, Ashley, because it might not come again.'

There was something in the way that Mrs Denly's eyes gazed into the distance that made Ashley wonder who she was really talking about.

'Oh, and you can remake that display for me before school tomorrow, young man. I know what you were trying to do, but you don't get out of it that easily!'

MENTAL SWITCH-ON

When someone has a reputation for being badly behaved, how could they change the way people think about them? How do you feel when people who don't follow the rules still get rewards?

SO WHAT?

- What sentence might describe Ashley's 'usual look'?
- In what ways could Ashley's mum not be coping?
- What do you think Ashley would most like to do at the farm?
- Why was Ashley's heart beating so fast when he'd finished destroying the display?
- Who, other than Ashley, could Mrs Denly have been talking about when she looked into the distance?

PRAYER

When we let ourselves and others down,
help us to do better.
And when others let us down,
help us to understand and forgive them.
Amen

Follow the rules and you'll be fine

> **WHAT'S IT ABOUT?**
>
> How will Omar and the rest of the children respond to a health and safety talk at Vicarwood Farm?

The day finally came for the start of the farm visit. The coach was there bright and early, so the driver, Mick, was standing outside the door with a steaming mug of coffee in his hand by the time parents and children started arriving. They dumped their suitcases and bags in an ordered heap by the open boot and gathered beside the hedge at either side of the entrance gates, chattering together in small groups. Mrs Denly didn't look as much like a head teacher as usual, dressed as she was in walking boots, jeans and a fleece. She was still very much in command, though, handing out labels to each of the children so that the luggage would end up with the right person when they reached Derbyshire. Mr Piper would be in charge while Mrs Denly was away, and he was hunched over Mick's atlas, looking at the route to the farm with him, a thoughtful, slightly nervous look on his face. At least most of the difficult Year Six children would be away, he was thinking, but there was still plenty that could go wrong…

Omar wasn't sure whether he wanted his mum and dad to wait to see him off or not. It wasn't his first time away from home but he was very aware of the Year Sixes standing in big groups and laughing noisily. Somehow, that extra year made all the difference, and he wasn't sure how well he'd get on with them for a whole week. You could keep out of their way on the playground and in the corridors easily enough, but how safe would it be on a farm? Would there be adults around all the time—just in case?

His mum and dad stood quietly at the back of the crowd of parents and other relatives that had assembled by the hedge outside school. Omar gave his suitcase and backpack to the driver, keeping his carrier bag in his hand, and climbed on to the coach without any problem. He was relieved to see that there was an empty place next to Andrew, one of his best friends, and he flopped into it gratefully. Once he'd got his MP3 player out of the bag and plugged it into his ears, he began to feel more relaxed—so much so that he almost forgot to wave to his mum and dad as the coach lurched over the two speed bumps outside school and headed for the dual carriageway out of town.

The journey was a long one, broken only by a stop at the motorway services. Mrs Denly and Mr Thorpe, the Year Six teacher who had persuaded to leave his young family and come away for the week, led them carefully in a column of pairs through the automatic doors and over to the toilets. Omar and Andrew managed to keep out of any trouble with the older boys and were pleased to meet up outside the Gents with Mr Thorpe. A few minutes later, Ashley had to be helped out of the shop by his sharp-eyed teacher, having ignored the instruction to stay in the main concourse while they waited for

Mrs Denly and the last of the girls to return. The two teaching assistants, Mrs Kitchen and Miss Shabani, brought up the rear as they all processed back to the coach, where Mick was waiting to release the door catch and let them in. Ashley had to wait until last because of his excursion to the shop, and he glared meaningfully at Omar as he placed his hand on the rail beside the steps. Omar noticed that Mr Thorpe had a hand wrapped firmly around Ashley's wrist, but he didn't think the teacher was aware of the stares that were being directed at them all. Mr Thorpe looked as though he was thinking about the long week that stretched before him.

As they left the motorway, Omar and Andrew noticed that the road was getting gradually more hilly, with the landscape changing, too. The hedges and fences that they'd seen up to now were gradually replaced by walls made from big stones that looked as if they had simply been piled up like long, thin mounds. They were nothing like the walls at home, which were made mostly from bricks fastened together with mortar, but they obviously did the job because the cows and sheep beyond them had not escaped yet.

As the morning drew on, the roads narrowed so much that the coach had to stop every now and again to let cars and tractors crawl by from the opposite direction. It was nearly lunch time when Mick steered the coach expertly off the road through a narrow stone gateway and into a dusty, stone-surfaced yard. As the children piled off the coach, they saw before them the farmhouse and a collection of barns, tractor sheds and cow loose boxes, with half-doors along the front. Next to the gate stood a small wooden sign bearing the words 'Vicarwood Farm' in an old-fashioned font. They had arrived.

'What do you think you're looking at?' whispered Ashley. Omar's eyes dropped before he stole a glance at Andrew, who was next to him. His friend's reassuring smile encouraged him to reply, although he kept a note of respect in his voice.

'Nothing, Ashley.'

'Listen, please, boys,' said Mr Thorpe sternly. 'These next few minutes could save your lives this week.'

They were all gathered in the huge farmhouse lounge, and the people who ran the farm were explaining the rules. A man called Tony began talking about the dangers that could be found on farms, particularly those that the children might find at Vicarwood. He spoke very quietly in an accent that Omar found hard to understand at times, although it was very much like the one that his cousin from Yorkshire used when he came to visit. Tony didn't smile much, either, a fact that gave a hint of menace to what he was saying.

'You've got to remember that farm animals can be unpredictable,' he explained. 'They've got hard hooves or sharp teeth, and some of them are very big.' A few of the children exchanged nervous glances. 'But if you listen to the advice of the staff each time you do a piece of work, and you treat the animals with respect, then you should be all right. Keep away from any areas with signs warning you about danger,' Tony continued. 'There's a slurry lagoon behind the cubicle sheds, the building where the cows sleep in winter. That's a lake of cow poo to you—runny and smelly and very, very deep. It has a dry crust on top, but if you slipped through you'd drown, so it's very, very deadly, too.'

Tony went on to describe the dangers of tractors and other big machines, and told the children how they should keep well out of the way when any of them was working. 'Remember,' he added, 'the driver or operator can't always see you, so take care of your own safety by thinking ahead all the time about what might happen, then try to make sure it doesn't. We want you to be safe and enjoy your stay here.'

Tony then led them all up the main staircase on to a huge landing where five dormitory bedroom doorways surrounded them, offering tantalising glimpses of bunk beds, washbasins and showers. They had climbed the stone stairs to get there, chattering excitedly and looking around as they did so. Tony's colleague, the other farm supervisor, now introduced herself to the group, leaning casually on the doorframe of one of the dormitories and smiling gently.

'My name's Nicky,' she said, 'and I'll tell you about the emergency evacuation procedure for the farmhouse.' She went on to tell the children and school staff about how they would safely clear the building if the fire alarm sounded. They would assemble in the farmyard, having followed all the green 'running man' signs, walking all the way.

'We're going to have a practice drill now,' she continued, 'so that you will know what the alarm sounds like, and so that you're clear about where to go.'

'And nobody's going to speak,' added Tony, looking around at each pair of eyes watching him. 'If anyone speaks, we'll do it again, and again, until you get it right.'

Omar noticed that Mr Thorpe caught Mrs Kitchen's eye at this point, with a look that said, 'I'll believe it when I see it.' The children were allocated temporarily to one of the dormitories and the teachers went to their own smaller bedrooms down a narrow corridor, ready to listen for the alarm.

Omar and Andrew sat on the bottom bunk in their dormitory and waited nervously. As soon as the sirens started, they jumped to their feet and hurried towards the staircase, joining with the silent river of children that was pouring across the landing carpet and down towards the front door. They noticed Tony standing at the bottom of the stairs, watching intently as everyone passed him. Nicky was waiting just outside the front door, standing on the lawn with her back to the garden, and she smiled encouragingly at the two boys as they turned smoothly to the right and headed through the gate into the farmyard. The assembly point was well away from the house, by a dry stone wall that bordered one of the lush green fields next to the farm. Omar was impressed and he could tell that Mrs Denly was, too. The children hardly ever moved this quietly or calmly at school. The head teacher smiled warmly at the rest of the staff when they joined the silent group, while Nicky read out the list of names to check that everyone was accounted for. It was Tony who spoilt the moment.

'It's a pity somebody spoke,' he said quietly, 'because I'm sure I warned you.' He turned his gaze towards Ashley, who thought briefly about arguing before looking guiltily down at the ground. 'So we'll do it again, until you all do as I've asked.'

Everyone turned to retrace their steps and repeat the exercise, with a number of the Year Sixes glaring at Ashley, who managed to avoid most of the looks. 'It's like I said,' Tony continued as they climbed the staircase for what everyone hoped would be the last time. 'Follow the rules and you'll be fine!'

MENTAL SWITCH-ON

Why do we have rules? Why is it important to follow them? What do the words 'health and safety' mean to pupils in a school? In what ways might a farm be a dangerous place to visit?

SO WHAT?

- What makes Year Sixes different?
- What might Omar's mum and dad have been thinking as the coach drove away?

- Why was Mr Thorpe thinking that it would be a long week?
- How do you think the children were feeling about the farm after all the health and safety warnings?
- Why do you think Ashley didn't argue with Tony?

PRAYER

Thank you for the rules that guide our lives,
thank you for the people who are wise enough to make them,
and thank you for the security we feel when we keep them.
Amen

Sometimes it's good to give something up

> **WHAT'S IT ABOUT?**
>
> Will Zara be able to sleep in the same dormitory as her best friend Alexia?

As soon as all the health and safety procedures had been completed, the children were taken by Tony and Nicky back to the main hallway by the front door where their luggage was piled up. Everyone had to collect their labelled suitcases and bags and then carry them up to the right dormitory. Each room held a maximum of either four or six children, and a plan had been drawn up back at school by Mr Thorpe to show where everyone would sleep. Obviously there were separate boys' and girls' rooms, with the numbers of Year Fives and Year Sixes working out just right to allow year groups not to be mixed.

Zara and Alexia were both in their last year at Winding Way Primary School, and they were proud of the fact that they'd been best friends since they'd first sat on the carpet together in Reception all those years ago. What had begun with occasional smiles and hand-holding on trips now included memories of birthday parties, sleepovers and, more recently, occasional trips to town, when they would wander happily through the mall, window shopping. When the dormitory plan had been drawn up, they had hoped and hoped that they could be together, and Mr Thorpe had been able to fit them into the same room quite easily, as the Winding Way group was not quite filling the farmhouse. There were 26 children's beds altogether, in five dormitories, and the numbers in their group meant that the seven Year Six girls fitted into two rooms, which had six and four beds in each. The three Year Five girls almost filled another four-bed room, and the five boys from Year Five were in a six-bed room. That left the five Year Six boys to occupy the last six-bed dormitory at the top of the stairs in the second-floor attic, conveniently next to the male staff bedroom.

The children were just about to start carrying their cases and bags up the steep stone staircase when a rather harassed Mr Thorpe appeared through the kitchen doorway. He took his glasses off and rubbed his eyes, gave a heavy sigh, dragged his hand down the side of his face and across his mouth, then returned his glasses before pulling a piece of folded white paper from his shirt pocket.

'I'm afraid we've got a problem with the dormitories,' he announced as he unfolded the paper. 'Unfortunately, Tony's just told me there's some building work planned for one of the four-bed dormitories and we can't use it this week.'

Mrs Denly put her suitcase and rucksack back on to the floor and walked up to Mr Thorpe. 'That shouldn't be a problem,' she said optimistically. 'We can just swap two of the Year Six girls back into the six-bed room, and one of them can join the Year Five girls in their four-bed room.'

'Yes, I'd thought of that,' agreed Mr Thorpe, 'but I don't like going back on a promise to the girls, and we had said that we wouldn't mix the year groups up.'

Zara exchanged a quick glance with Alexia, who was also listening to the conversation with interest. In fact, when she looked around, she noticed that all the older girls had gathered together behind Mrs Denly. Some still had their luggage gripped in their hands, while others had left their bags in the pile. Several of them had begun to whisper to each other.

'I think the best thing is for me to meet with the Year Six girls in the lounge while you get all the others settled into their dormitories,' Mrs Denly said firmly. Mr Thorpe didn't look too sure about this, but he seemed pleased that something had been decided. With the help of the two teaching assistants, Miss Shabani and Mrs Kitchen, he ushered all the other children up the staircase. When they'd gone, the seven girls followed Mrs Denly through a large door into an enormous lounge, thickly carpeted in red and green and crammed with an enormous variety of sofas and easy chairs in all sorts of styles and colours. Jade-Marie, who always seemed to believe that she should be in charge at times like this, sat importantly next to the head teacher on the largest sofa and then told everyone else where she felt they ought to sit.

'Just find somewhere, everyone,' Mrs Denly added, somehow managing to look irritated and encouraging at the same time. 'It seems that I'm looking for a volunteer,' she continued, looking significantly round the circle of faces in front of her, 'because seven's an odd number. One of you will have to join the Year Fives in their room, I'm afraid.'

'My mum wrote to you about me having to be with Kirsty,' Jade-Marie said, without pausing to think. 'We've had loads of sleepovers and I might get an asthma attack if I get nervous in the night.'

She smiled meaningfully at Kirsty, who looked rather embarrassed but quickly dropped her gaze so that no one else could see what she was thinking. Zara looked quickly sideways to where Holly and Tamzin were sitting together, squeezed tightly into a wide armchair. She remembered how upset Tamzin had been when her mum died last year, and how close she'd got to Holly while she was trying to get over her awful loss. That left Ellie—sitting on her own, as usual, with that awkward look on her face, and her arms folded tightly across her chest. Zara tried to imagine her in a room with the Year Five girls, but her heart sank immediately out of concern for them. There was only one thing for it. Without looking at Alexia, the best friend who, she knew, was so much looking forward to sharing the excitement of these farmyard nights with her, she cleared her voice and spoke up.

'I'll move, Mrs Denly,' she offered.

'That's lovely of you, Zara,' replied Mrs Denly without pausing. She was obviously relieved not to have to ask someone, especially with the promise that Mr Thorpe had made earlier. For some reason, Zara couldn't bring herself to look at Alexia as they filed out of the lounge to collect their gear and make the trek upstairs to unpack. She was aware of some very positive comments directed her way. 'Nice one, Zara.' 'Well done.' 'Thanks for volunteering.' It would have been nice if Ellie had thanked her for offering to drop out of the Year Six room, but hers was the only voice that Zara didn't hear as they climbed to the first floor.

'I'll miss you.' This last comment came from Alexia. 'I was about to say something myself but you got in first,' she added, sniggering. At least Zara didn't have to worry about what Alexia thought of her actions. Mrs Denly seemed pleased, too, and that always felt good.

Zara dragged her heavy black suitcase into the four-bed dormitory at the top of the first staircase, while Mrs Denly held the door and smiled encouragingly at everyone, did the introductions and then hurried away. Zara heaved the suitcase on to the bed to begin unpacking. The Year Five girls were already well into stowing their clothes in the long chest of drawers under the window. When she peered into the en-suite shower room, she saw that they'd lined up their toothbrushes, flannels, shampoos and other washing paraphernalia along the glass shelf. It occurred to Zara that she knew Charlotte (or Charlie, as her friends called her) from netball club, and she noticed that the girl had no one to share her bunk with.

'Can I have this bed?' she asked carefully, pointing to the upper bunk, which didn't have any pyjamas on the pillow.

'If you like,' replied Charlie, without smiling. The other two girls exchanged meaningful glances, although Zara didn't know them well enough to be able to guess what they were saying with their eyes.

It was while Zara was quietly unpacking her clothes that Mr Thorpe tapped politely on their door, asked if they were all decent, and then put his head round.

'I've got some news, Zara,' he said, beaming all over his face. 'The builders have just rung up to say that they can't come this week after all. That means we can go back to our original arrangements.'

Zara's heart leapt and she began repacking her suitcase straight away.

'I hope you three aren't too upset about missing out on Zara's company,' he went on, looking expectantly at them.

Zara didn't hear their reply, as she was already heading through the doorway to find Alexia and the rest of the gang. She passed Mrs Denly on the landing and explained what had happened.

'I would have gone through with it, Mrs Denly, if the builders had come,' she said.

She was certain that changing rooms would have spoilt

her week, but she could only guess how good she'd have felt for being helpful. Mrs Denly seemed to sum up what she was thinking with her reply.

'Sometimes it's good to give something up!'

MENTAL SWITCH-ON

What is a dormitory? Where might people sleep in a shared bedroom? How does it feel to sleep in a room with people you don't know? What makes sleepovers so much fun?

SO WHAT?

- What makes someone a good friend?
- How can body language, like Mr Thorpe taking his glasses off and wiping his face, help us to understand how people are feeling?
- Why is it important for people to keep promises whenever possible?
- What do you think Kirsty was thinking when Jade-Marie looked at her in the lounge?
- How would Zara have felt if she'd had to go through with her offer?

PRAYER

Thank you for friendship,
for the chance to be there for each other,
and for the joy of knowing we are not alone.
Amen

Next time, think about it first, please

> ### WHAT'S IT ABOUT?
> On the first night of the visit, Mr Thorpe wonders if it's just tiredness that's affecting Martin's behaviour.

Martin had put all his clothes away in his own drawer on the window side of the Year Five boys' dormitory. He'd put his washbag in the shower room and his wellingtons in the row under the window. He surveyed the room before flinging himself contentedly on to the bottom bunk nearest the door and sighing joyfully. This was brilliant. A whole week away from home lay before him, full of promise. Andrew and Errol were squabbling over a towel and where it was going to hang, but all Martin could really hear were the sounds of the farmyard drifting in through the open window—the contented grunting of the huge pigs in their sty, the shrill call of a cockerel every few minutes, the low moaning of the brown and white cows waiting to be milked. Then came the unmistakable roar of a tractor as it turned off the tarmac road and on to the grey cobbles.

Martin swung his legs over the side of the bed and ran across to look at the machine below him outside. It was mostly red, with a mud-spattered grey engine, wheels and a combination of steel arms, chains and a drawbar at the back. Whenever Martin had seen tractors before, this had been the bit that fascinated him. This was what allowed the tractor to lift and pull so many different types of implement, most of which he didn't even know the names of. All that power and strength! He'd love to have a go at driving one some day. Maybe he'd even get a chance this week.

As he was thinking this, he saw the driver, a tall man in a boiler suit, swing open the grey door and jump down on to the stone-covered yard with a resounding clatter. This must be the farmer they'd heard about from Mrs Denly before they came. Martin couldn't remember his name, but he looked a bit severe as he marched off towards a sliding door on the far side of the yard and disappeared through it. An engine started up soon after he'd gone into the shed, and Martin could hear the cows banging about in a large shed that made up one side of the brick buildings opposite the farmhouse. He could also hear a rhythmic clicking, a bit like a group of huge clocks marking the passage of time together. He made a mental note to ask a question later when he saw someone who might know what was going on in there.

The children had their tea in the huge dining-room, chattering excitedly as they sat around the three large wooden tables. All the staff were sitting at a table of their own in the corner. They took it in turns to move around the room, answering a question here or asking someone to calm down a bit there. Once the dishes had been cleared away, Nicky, one of the farm's two supervisors, stood up and got everyone quiet.

'It's time for your evening jobs now,' she said, 'so we need to put you into your work groups for the week. I've spoken to your teachers and they think it would be a very good idea to mix up the Year Fives and Year Sixes.'

This news brought a sudden babble of conversation from all of the tables, and Nicky had to put her hand in the air—the agreed signal for getting the children's attention. Gradually, they all followed her lead, so that she could continue. 'When I read each name out, I'd like you to go and stand with your staff leader. There are five groups of four, but sometimes two groups will do an activity together because we usually have three activities at a time. We'll rotate which group does what for most of the jobs, but you'll have other tasks for the whole week so that you get to know them well.'

Each group was to have two boys and two girls in it, so, with five boys from Year Five and the same number from Year Six, it was clearly going to be one from each year in every group. Martin's name was called straight away, as the Year Five boy in Work Group One, but, he wondered, who would he be partnered with…?

The children returned from their evening jobs tired and, for the most part, very dirty. Groups One and Two had been putting the cows back into the field after milking, and cleaning out the collecting yard where the cows gathered each morning and afternoon while they waited to be milked. Groups Three and Four had been feeding the pigs and putting extra straw bedding in the sties. Group Five had been locking the chickens, ducks and geese away in their various sheds, houses and runs to keep them safe from the foxes that Tony told them would come prowling around the farm at night.

Martin hosed the cow muck off his wellies and leggings before putting them untidily in his allocated place in the drying room. His group leader, Mrs Kitchen, was waiting by the door into the main farmhouse, and she sent him back to straighten his wellies and turn his leggings right way out so that they would dry. Martin muttered something inaudible as he stomped back to sort things out, but Mrs Kitchen let it go because she could see how tired all the children were after their very long day. She could always talk to him about his attitude later, when he wouldn't be so sensitive, and when he might even listen to what she was saying.

Martin went up to his room and showered as quickly as he could, before the others got back from their work. Mrs Denly had said that they must all have a shower every night, so he felt a bit more cheerful being ahead of everyone else. It was diary time once he had dressed, allowing him to lie on his bunk and write about the day so far. He hated blank pieces of paper. It was so hard to get started, but he found that once he'd got a few words down, the rest started to flow. No one had been near a tractor yet, which was his biggest disappointment, but he had managed to find out what the noise in the yard had been, earlier. Mr Turner, the farmer, had shown Martin's group into the milking parlour as the last group of cows was being milked, and they'd all seen the stainless steel tubes with black rubber linings that sucked the milk out of each cow's four teats, accompanied by a loud, rhythmic clicking caused by the vacuum pump on the wall.

After supper and a chapter of a storybook in the lounge, all the children went up to their beds. Mrs Denly and Mr Thorpe did their rounds with the medicines that some of the children needed, and then it was lights out and off to sleep. Well, that was the theory, but Martin had very different ideas.

The staff were relaxing around the kitchen table over a cup of coffee when they heard the first sounds of disruption from upstairs. Mr Thorpe offered to go and see what the problem was, and, when he traced the sound of running to the Year Five boys' dormitory, he wasn't entirely surprised. He knocked briefly, told the boys that he was coming in and then opened the door. The sight that met his eyes genuinely surprised him. Martin was standing statue-like in the middle of the floor, his diary in his hands, while Andrew on the top bunk opposite was poised to throw a rolled-up sock at the upturned bin behind him.

'What on earth do you think you're doing?' demanded Mr Thorpe, barely able to control himself.

'We're playing cricket,' answered Martin matter-of-factly, waving his diary as he went on to explain that it was the bat, with the bin as the wicket.

'Didn't Mrs Denly and I make it perfectly clear that you were to go to sleep?' replied Mr Thorpe. 'Perhaps a little bit of quiet talking while you went off, we said. That does not include playing cricket. Now get into bed, all of you, and don't let me hear another sound from here.'

Once the boys were settled under the covers again, the teacher closed the door just forcefully enough to underline his point and returned to finish his coffee before it got too cold to be satisfying.

Mr Thorpe was enjoying a blissful dream about scoring the winning goal in the World Cup Final when he suddenly returned to reality and to the sound that had awoken him. He grabbed his watch from the bedside table, pushing the button that lit up the dial. Five past twelve. What now? He threw on a T-shirt and jeans, pulled his trainers on to his feet and went out to the landing. All was quiet in the Year Six boys' room, so he made his way cautiously down the stairs, finding it hard to control his legs, half-asleep as he was. This was unbelievable. It was Martin and his lot again.

'Now what?' he shouted, bursting through the door, very much aware that he was showing his anger in doing so. This time it was just Martin, standing by the chest of drawers, trying without success to conceal the biscuits he'd smuggled out of supper and the Nintendo DS that he'd been playing with a moment before. The other boys were asleep as far as Mr Thorpe could tell, so he summoned the culprit out of the room and on to the landing.

'What is going on?' demanded the teacher in a fierce whisper. 'I can't believe the way you're behaving. You were so keen to come, and yet you choose to constantly disobey me. We all need our sleep, you know, me included. Now give me that Nintendo and get back to bed.'

Martin studied the floorboards between his bare feet, and decided to try to explain. 'It was fine till I got put in a group with Ashley.'

Mr Thorpe's tired face lit up at this. It explained what Mrs Kitchen had said to him earlier about Martin's unusual behaviour before supper.

'That's no excuse, Martin,' he said, his voice a little warmer than before. 'You could have said something to any of us. As it happens, Mrs Denly and I chose you to work with Ashley because we think you're strong enough to stand up to him, especially with a bit of help from Mrs Kitchen. Now, how are you going to put it right?'

Martin thought for a moment and then suggested a number of things that he thought would persuade Mr Thorpe that he was really sorry for what he'd done, and would help him to behave better in future. Luckily enough, Mr Thorpe agreed with him, although, as he closed the dormitory door, he did offer one final piece of advice.

'Next time, think about it first, please!'

MENTAL SWITCH-ON

How does it feel to be really angry? What happens to your body and your voice? How can you tell that a teacher is angry? What makes a teacher most angry?

SO WHAT?

- What do you think it was about the farmer that made him look severe to Martin?
- Why do you think the teachers wanted to mix up the year groups?
- How would Martin's feelings be different later if Mrs Kitchen spoke to him about his behaviour then?
- How do you feel about adults being angry with children?
- What consequences do you think Martin thought of to show Mr Thorpe that he was really sorry?

PRAYER

Anger is hard to live with,
whether it's mine or someone else's,
but at those times when it helps to make things right,
may I accept and understand it.
Amen

6

Pass the salt, please, mate

> ### WHAT'S IT ABOUT?
> Sam doesn't really get Omar, so how will things turn out when they have to work together on the farm?

On the first morning, it was a bit of a shock for everyone when Mr Thorpe, mug of tea in hand, visited all the dormitories with a jaunty knock and a wake-up call.

'Time to get up, all of you,' he said cheerily to the occupants of each room. 'Early morning jobs are waiting.'

Sam rolled over with a groan and tried to shut out the noise. He couldn't remember what time he'd finally got off to sleep, but he clearly remembered seeing 1:30 blazing out on his watch display. He decided to wait just a bit longer before getting up. He must have drifted off again because, the next thing he knew, Jon was rocking him violently by the shoulder and telling him that the sink in the shower room was free.

'Come on, we're all dressed and ready,' said Jon by way of encouragement. 'Mr Thorpe'll be back in a minute and you'll be for it if you're not out of bed.'

Five minutes later, rubbing the sleep out of his eyes, Sam

was standing on the landing with the other children, ready to join the rest of Group Two for their morning tasks. He knew Kirsty because she was in his Year Six maths group, and he didn't mind Lara, the Year Five girl, because he hadn't found her annoying when they'd fed the pigs together last night after tea. On the other hand, the fourth member of the group was Omar from Year Five, who had been quite strange last night. When the others had gone into the pigsty with the buckets of barley meal, he'd hovered outside the gate, looking anxious. Mrs Denly had told him that he could just watch if he wanted, and she'd been really kind about his wimpish behaviour. Perhaps he'd had a bad experience with pigs before, or maybe he just couldn't bear the smell. Personally, Sam quite liked pigs—the way they grunted and seemed to be smiling all the time. OK, the big mother sows were a bit scary, being so big and pushing and shoving so hard, but the piglets were brilliant, scurrying about with their little pink ears flopping up and down.

Mrs Denly bounded down the stairs with her usual enthusiasm and gathered her group around her. 'Good morning, everyone. I hope you all slept well.'

They all nodded quietly, although, judging from their faces, it looked to Sam as if he wasn't the only one who had struggled to sleep.

'This morning we are meeting Mrs Turner, the farmer's wife, who's going to show us how to collect the eggs.'

Once they'd got their wellingtons on, they headed off to the farmhouse. It was warm enough, even at 7.30, for them not to need their coats, although Sam was pleased he'd put his fleece on. The girls walked together in front with Mrs Denly, so Sam found himself next to Omar when they reached the small iron hand-gate by the farmhouse back door, but neither of them spoke. A small woman in jeans and a thick brown woolly jumper that matched her untidy hair was waiting for them. She smiled warmly when they reached the gate, and led them off to the barn, where a row of paper sacks were lined up against the wall. There was a picture of a chicken printed on the outside of each one, with the words 'Layers Pellets' underneath.

'You can work in pairs,' she said. 'You'll need a bucket each and a scoop. They're over there if you'd like to help yourselves.' Sam followed her pointing finger and saw the equipment in a corner, sitting on a dusty table. There were also some empty cardboard egg boxes on the table, piled up against the brick wall behind.

'If you fill your bucket with pellets using the scoop, you'll be ready to come out into the orchard,' explained Mrs Turner. 'Why don't you girls go with Mrs Denly?' she went on. 'She knows what you need to do. The boys can come with me.'

Sam used the scoop to fill the bucket that Omar was holding, and they set off through the back door of the barn into a grass paddock with trees dotted around almost as far as the eye could see. As they walked past the trees, Sam could see big green apples dangling from the branches. Some of the trees were covered in a similar way with small, crunchy-looking pears.

'I could murder one of those,' he said to Omar, forgetting for a moment that they weren't talking.

'Me too,' replied Omar with a cautious smile, his bright white teeth gleaming brilliantly against his light brown skin.

They soon reached a chicken house, about the same size as a garden shed, with creosoted wooden walls and a sloping felted roof. At one end of the shed, a small sliding door opened into a wire mesh run, but there was also another door, with a ramp, that would allow the chickens to roam free in the orchard when it was open. Running the full length of the wall nearest to them, Sam could see, there was a long wooden box, fastened about half way up the side. It had a felted lid, a bit like the roof, which was hinged so that it could be lifted up easily.

Mrs Turner pulled a rusty steel nail out of a fastener and raised the lid carefully. Sam could see one of the brown chickens sitting in the box, but, when it saw them all standing there, it scrambled quickly to its feet and hurried back into the main part of the shed through a small opening, clucking in alarm. There were several of these openings into the shed, so that the chickens could move easily in and out of the box. It was lined with bright yellow straw, with a few small brown and white feathers mixed in. And there, nestled amid the straw where the chicken had been sitting, Sam could see three large brown eggs. As he looked down the box, he noticed more clumps of eggs.

'This is a nest box,' explained Mrs Turner, 'and if we keep taking the eggs every day, the chickens keep on laying. What you need to do is to open the outside door, feed the chickens in this trough and then put the eggs carefully in your bucket. It works well if you leave a few pellets in the bottom to stop the eggs from rolling around too much. I'll go and fetch some water for them.'

She lowered the lid carefully and hurried off, back towards the barn. Sam looked at Omar. 'Why don't you open the door and I'll pour the pellets into the trough,' he said.

Omar nodded and walked round to the front of the shed. He pulled the door up carefully and stood back quickly as the chickens cautiously made their way down the ramp and into the lush green grass of the orchard. They soon gained enough confidence to hurry over to the trough and begin pecking busily at the pellets.

'They're like the ones I give my rabbit,' Omar said, watching the chickens intently.

'I had a rabbit once, but it died,' Sam responded. 'My dad said a fox must've broken into the hutch and nabbed it.'

He stood quietly for a moment, remembering his rabbit with affection, and then snapped out of it. He moved back to the box and lifted the lid, which was much heavier than it had looked in Mrs Turner's hands. The bucket was by his feet, but he couldn't bend down to reach the clutch of eggs and place them on the layer of unused pellets because he couldn't hold the lid with one hand.

'You'll have to help me, Omar,' he said, his voice cracking slightly with the strain of holding the lid.

Omar trotted quickly across the grass to hold the heavy wooden cover up against the side of the chicken house. 'You collect the eggs,' he suggested as he did so.

Sam took the bucket by its handle in one hand and walked as quickly as he could down beside the nesting box, lifting each egg out of the straw and placing it, as delicately as possible, in the bucket. In no time at all, he had gathered 20 eggs. There was some clucking from inside the shed, but the chickens seemed to accept his robbery of their eggs remarkably well. Perhaps they were used to it by now, he thought.

As soon as he had collected the last egg, Mrs Turner reappeared with two enormous buckets of water, sloshing some of the contents on to the grass as she plonked them down beside the round metal water troughs. 'You two have been very busy,' she commented, looking at the eggs in their bucket. 'Nice teamwork.'

All the children were back in the dining-room half an hour later, their outdoor clothes left in the drying-room and their hands and faces safely washed after their early jobs. Sam had been to the hatch, which opened into the kitchen, to get rid of his cereal bowl and collect his boiled eggs and toast.

'I thought you'd have had the sausages,' said Kirsty as he returned to his table and sat down.

Sam looked sideways at Omar, who was sitting in the next place, already chopping the top off one of his eggs with a knife. They'd talked about the pigs on the way back from the barn, and how Omar felt about them because of his religion, Islam. Besides, they'd worked hard to get these eggs back to the kitchen in time for breakfast.

'I thought I'd give the sausages a miss this week,' Sam told Kirsty, smiling to himself as he said it. And then, looking at Omar, he said, 'Pass the salt, please, mate!'

MENTAL SWITCH-ON

What do you find annoying about other people? How can you get to know people better when you first meet them? How important are first impressions? Are they always right?

SO WHAT?

- How does Sam feel about Omar after the incident with the pigs the previous evening?
- How might Sam have described the other children's faces as they were waiting to go outside to their task?
- Why do you think Omar smiled when Sam drew his attention to the pears? What do you think made him cautious about doing so?
- In what ways might it help us to remember pets or people who have died?
- What does Sam's comment about sausages near the end of the story tell you about what he thinks of Omar now?

PRAYER

May we take the time to get to know others;
may we make the effort to understand their views and ideas,
so that we can all share our lives in harmony and peace.
Amen

Never be afraid to say you don't know

> ### WHAT'S IT ABOUT?
>
> Holly doesn't really know what it is that Mr Turner the farmer wants her to fetch from the tool shed, but she decides to keep quiet about it.

Holly was on table-wiping duty after breakfast, so she wrung out the cloth again and ran it backwards and forwards over the wood-pattern surface of the last table in the dining-room before returning it to the kitchen hatch, where the lady in the blue overall took it from her with a smile and a jolly 'Thank you, duck.' With her jobs done, she was able to go to the drying-room to get her wellies and outdoor clothes on, along with the rest of Group Three. Miss Shabani was just pulling on her long flowery rubber boots when she arrived.

'We're cleaning out the collecting yard,' she explained, pulling a face as she did so. 'I think it's a bit smelly. You don't mind, do you?'

Holly shook her head. Now that she was in Year Six, her dad had let her start cycling down to her local stables from the end of the summer holidays, and she was used to dealing with horse muck. This couldn't be very different, could it?

'I think the farm smells quite nice really,' she said, tugging her leggings over her wellies and wishing she'd put them on first.

'You must be mad,' said Zara, one of the other Year Sixes in the group. 'I can't stand it.'

'Well, I think it grows on you,' said Jon, 'because I can hardly smell it now, and we've only been here a day.'

Andrew, the Year Five, was the only one who hadn't said anything yet, but he was struggling with the zip on his waterproof coat and didn't seem to be listening. 'Miss, why have we got to wear our coats on a warm day like this?' he asked.

'It's for health and safety reasons, so that you can hose and brush them down after work. It's to keep bacteria off your normal clothes.'

When they were all wrapped up in their protective gear, they trudged across the farmyard to the milking parlour, where they could hear the sound of whistling drifting through the open door.

Mr Turner, the farmer, put his head round the door when he heard them approaching and came out to meet them in a long orange waterproof apron, green wellies and a very worn and dirty flat cap. It was soon clear to Holly that he wasn't a very smiley kind of man, although he seemed nice enough.

'You've come to clean out the collecting yard, then,' he said, rather gruffly.

'That's right,' said Miss Shabani, 'according to the rota in the farmhouse.'

'Well, the first thing yer need to do is to help me get the cars back across the road into the fields they're grazing at the moment,' he explained. 'Let me just hang me apron up and ah'll be with yer.'

'What does he mean about cars?' whispered Zara to Miss Shabani.

'I think it's Mr Turner's Derbyshire accent,' replied the teaching assistant quietly. 'It's his way of saying cows.'

Mr Turner soon reappeared, hurrying across the yard to the big gate that kept the cows in the collecting yard. As he swung to open it, the large brown-and-white cattle began to walk steadily out into the main yard, nose to tail, rather like huge children heading out on to the playing field at lunch time, although much more slowly. Every now and again, there was a bit of a scuffle as one of the cows tried to push in front of the others, but mostly it was an orderly procession.

A cow stopped to moo loudly, right beside Holly. The sound made her bones vibrate with its volume, but she wasn't really scared. Two or three raised their tails while gurgling streams of runny green muck ran out on to the concreted part of the yard with a plop-plop-plopping sound, but otherwise the task was uneventful. The herd gathered at the gates to the farmyard while Mr Turner opened them. Then he stood on the road in case any traffic came, and Group Three walked carefully behind the cows, patting them on the rump if they stopped and generally ushering them across the road. Andrew had been given a shovel by Mr Turner as they were walking across the yard, and it now became clear what that was for.

'Yer can shift that off the road if yer like,' said Mr Turner, nodding at a large green pat of steaming muck on the tarmac. 'Ah'll watch fer cars.'

This time everyone assumed the farmer meant cars rather than cows, but they weren't completely sure.

Once the herd had been secured in the field across the road, and the cows were busily grazing at the lush green grass, the group of children followed the adults back to the empty collecting yard, where Mr Turner gave them their next instructions.

'Now, there's a wheelbarrow here, yer need to get a shovel each from the end of the parlour, and one of yer will need to fetch the squeegee.'

Mr Turner looked directly at Holly with steely blue eyes. 'That can be you,' he added. 'It's in the tool shed over there. Ah've bin mendin' it.'

As she set off in the direction of his pointing finger, Mr Turner asked, 'Do yer know what a squeegee is?'

'Oh yes,' she replied, without hesitating for a moment. However, she wasn't anything like as confident as she sounded. She hadn't a clue what he was talking about, but she was fairly sure that she would be able to work it out when she reached the tool shed. How hard could it be?

The tool shed was very dark and dusty, with the smell of oil hanging in the air. As her eyes grew accustomed to the dark, Holly began to make out the shapes of some of the tools. Some were hanging from the walls, some were lying on the workbench and others were hanging from the old wooden beams that held the roof up, but nothing looked as though it might be a squeegee. She recognised forks and spades, pickaxes and brooms, but there were so many other tools and pieces of equipment that she hadn't seen before.

What should she do? Holly was working her way through the options when Jon suddenly appeared in the doorway.

'Are you all right, Holly?' he asked, his voice full of concern. 'We were beginning to think something had happened to you. Have you found the squeegee yet?'

'Erm, yes, I was just looking round the other tools while I was here to see if anything else might be useful,' she answered, not very convincingly.

'Well, we're ready to get started, so hurry up, will you.' With that, Jon hurried off back to the collecting yard, leaving Holly still wondering what to do.

If she went back with the wrong tool, they'd all laugh at her, and if she went back empty-handed they'd all ask her where the squeegee was. Either way, she'd have to admit that she didn't really know what a squeegee was. Why on earth had she said that she did in the first place?

Miss Shabani appeared next and put a reassuring arm round Holly's shoulder. 'Have you found that squeegee yet?' she asked. 'We could really do with it, I think. The shovels are a bit slow.'

Holly thought for a second or two before explaining to Miss Shabani what her dilemma was.

'Why don't you go and tell Mr Turner that you didn't know after all, and could he describe it to you?' suggested Miss Shabani. 'What's the worst that can happen?'

She was right, thought Holly. It was the obvious thing to do.

Mr Turner was lovely about it when she told him. He took his cap off, scratched at his thinning grey hair and chuckled heartily.

'Ah didn't think yer knew, but ah'm pleased yer've come and told me. It isn't obvious from the name, is it? Right, it's made of a curved piece of corrugated steel with a rubber blade on the bottom, and it's fastened to a broom handle so that you can push the slurry along into one place for the people with shovels to pick up.' Holly's face lit up, because she knew exactly where that was in the tool shed. Well, she thought she'd seen something like it, anyway.

'I won't be long,' she said, hurrying off towards the tool shed again—and she wasn't. Within minutes Holly was pushing her squeegee happily through the sloppy mixture of cow muck and urine on the collecting yard floor, leaving wide strips of cleaner, dryer concrete in her wake.

'What have yer learnt, duck?' asked Mr Turner as she leaned proudly on the handle while the others busily filled the wheelbarrow.

Holly gave it a moment's thought before answering, 'Never be afraid to say you don't know!'

MENTAL SWITCH-ON

What's the worst smell you can think of? How would you describe it? How do you feel when someone says something you don't understand, even though you think you should?

SO WHAT?

- How do you think parents decide what their children can safely do at a certain age?
- Why did Miss Shabani speak quietly about Mr Turner's accent?
- Why did Holly say that she knew what a squeegee was?
- When did you last reassure someone? How did it feel?
- What is Holly proud about at the end of the story?

PRAYER

Teach us that honesty is usually the best choice,
give us the courage to take the right path,
and help us to understand that you accept us as we are.
Amen

8

Sorry, but it was me

WHAT'S IT ABOUT?

What will Marcel decide to do about a mistake with the pigs?

It was Group Four's turn to work with the pigs this morning, so they had to meet Tony, one of the two farm supervisors, at the barn. Mr Thorpe pointed out one piece of machinery that he recognised while they were waiting for Tony to arrive.

'In the corner there's a mill for rolling cereal grains like barley or oats, or sometimes wheat. Let's go and have a look.'

The children followed Mr Thorpe across to a large pair of steel wheels mounted in a frame, covered with a fine white dust. Above the wheels was a large wooden box, and there was a hole in the ceiling directly above it.

'What's that for, sir?' asked Harry.

Before the teacher could answer, Marcel jumped in knowledgeably. 'It's where the corn comes down into the hopper from upstairs.'

'Well done, Marcel,' Mr Thorpe said, looking suitably impressed. 'How do you know that?'

'When I went back to Poland this summer, I went to my grandad's farm, and he has one,' the Year Six boy explained. 'He keeps pigs, too.'

'I'll be looking to you for some of the answers later, then,' replied Mr Thorpe. Tony walked through the barn door at this point, so they turned their attention to him.

'Sorry I'm a bit late,' he said. 'I had trouble starting my car this morning. Now, you're on pig jobs, so you need two shovels, two forks and a wheelbarrow. You'll find them all in the corner over there.'

Tamzin and Jade-Marie, both in Year Six with Marcel, grabbed a fork each, leaving shovels for the two boys. Marcel knew Harry from football club, and he respected him for his skill and hard work. The girls he didn't know so well, although he did literacy with them back at school, when he wasn't having extra help. Marcel volunteered to push the wheelbarrow and dropped his shovel into it so that he would have both hands free to hold the handles. Mr Thorpe sauntered along behind the group, fiddling with his camera, as they headed for the pigsty.

The two pink mother pigs, with black spots splattered over their backs like paint, were looking up at the top of the brick wall as Marcel looked over at them. Each one had a pen of its own, each with a group of piglets wandering in and out of a low doorway at the back of their enclosure.

'These are Gloucester Old Spot pigs, a very old breed,' explained Tony, leaning against the wall. 'They are known for being good-natured and producing very tasty meat. They can also live outside quite happily, and we'll be putting them in the orchard for a while later in the autumn to clear up any fallen apples that we don't need. Does anyone know the word for a female pig?'

'Is it a sow?' asked Tamzin hesitantly.

'That's right—unless it hasn't had any piglets yet, in which case it's a gilt,' answered Tony. 'Your task this morning is to muck out the pigsty, so we've got to shut both the families into their outside run first. Then I can open the door at the side to let you in with the wheelbarrow.' He led them to the door, opened the top half and looked over it into the darkness. As there were no piglets near the door, he opened the bottom half and slipped in, closing it quickly behind him, but then looking back immediately at the group of children.

'I need a couple of volunteers to come and help now,' he said.

Marcel and Tamzin put their hands up and were allowed into the pigsty by Tony, who opened the door slightly for just long enough to let them through. The rest of the group gathered round the door, the children standing on tiptoe to see inside, and Mr Thorpe using his flash to get some good photos of the piglets darting excitedly around. Each one was about the size of a cat, but their jerky movements, flopping ears and delighted squeals were very far from catlike.

Marcel and Tamzin soon realised that Tony was pushing all the piglets outside to join their mums, first in the part of the sty nearest the door, and then from the further half, which they reached through another wooden half-door. Once each part of the sleeping quarters was empty, Tony closed a small metal gate to keep the pigs outside. The piglets were just too big to squeeze back between the bars, so it was now safe to open the double door fully so that the wheelbarrow could be wheeled in.

'Jade-Marie, why don't you take a turn now?' suggested Mr Thorpe, and she duly lifted the barrow and bumped it up the stone step into the sty, grunting with the effort. Everyone then got stuck into clearing the concrete floor of all the mucky wet straw that was scattered around. It smelt pretty strong, but, apart from a few wrinkled noses and the occasional cry of 'Pwoor', no one seemed to mind too much. They finished the first side and Tony took Harry off to tip the wheelbarrow on the muck heap in the corner of the farmyard, while the rest started clearing the second side.

'I don't know how anyone can eat pork or bacon when you see how gorgeous the piglets are,' said Jade-Marie while they were waiting for the wheelbarrow to return.

'If we didn't have farms, there wouldn't be any piglets to be gorgeous,' observed Mr Thorpe.

'And if they have a good life before they're killed, does it matter?' added Marcel.

'I think the world would be a worse place without sausages like the ones we had for breakfast this morning,' offered Tamzin.

'Well, I was happy enough with toast, thank you,' concluded Jade-Marie as Harry trundled the wheelbarrow back into the sty. Tony pointed out that it was now full of dry yellow barley straw, so that they could bed the sleeping areas of the sty again.

'If you drop the straw this side, we can clean the other side, shake the straw out in both of them and then do the outside areas.'

This they did, shooing each family of pigs into the sleeping area before opening the front wooden doors to allow access with the barrow. Within 15 minutes they had finished cleaning out the two outdoor areas, which were not as dirty as the inside ones. Jade-Marie fetched a broom from the barn to complete the finishing touches, and then Tamzin wheeled the barrow back to the barn, where the rest of them dropped their tools into it.

Tony joined them to explain briefly that he had to go back to the house early because the mechanic from the local garage had arrived to look at his car.

'Do you think you could keep an eye on the children for me, Mr Thorpe, while they open the gates to the living quarters to let the pigs back out?' he asked. 'Oh, and they could give them the kitchen scraps in those two buckets while they're at it.'

'No problem,' answered the teacher as Tony hurried off. 'Come on, you lot. Let's get the job done. Then we can go and get ourselves cleaned up.'

✪

The children from Group Four were sitting in the study room at the top of the farmhouse, doing sketches and oil pastels of pigs from a poster and some books, when they heard footsteps stomping up the staircase below. Tony suddenly appeared in the room, his face red with the effort of climbing.

'Who left the pigsty door open?' he asked sternly, looking at each of the children in turn.

'Why, what's 'appened?' asked Harry nervously.

'Half the pigs were out all over the yard, that's what,' said Tony unsmilingly. 'It's a wonder they didn't get on to the road and cause an accident.'

Mr Thorpe, who had clearly heard the commotion from his room next door, joined them. 'I'm very disappointed in you lot,' he said. 'I told you how important it was to shut everything properly, and I really thought the responsibility would do you good. You're in Year Six now—well, Year Five at least in your case, Harry. It's just not good enough.'

There was silence for a moment before Mr Thorpe asked if the children needed to help put the pigs back.

'No, it's OK, Mr and Mrs Turner have done that already,' explained Tony. 'I just want to know who forgot to close the front door.'

Marcel thought hard and tried to picture who'd been last out of the sty when they'd put the kitchen scraps in, but he couldn't. He looked around the room at the others, but they seemed just as confused.

'I agree with Tony,' said Mr Thorpe pointedly. 'You will all go without supper unless the culprit owns up. It's as simple as that.' Tony seemed pleased with the teacher's support, because, for the first time since he'd come upstairs, he seemed a little bit happier.

The more Marcel thought about it, the surer he was that he'd closed the back door when Mr Thorpe had asked him to, but he'd not been the one to fasten the front because he'd had an empty bucket in his hand when they came out. Still, someone had to speak out or none of them would get any supper. Summoning up all his courage, he raised his hand steadily and looked at Mr Thorpe, who met his gaze with more warmth than Marcel had expected.

'Sorry, but it was me!'

MENTAL SWITCH-ON

What happens when a member of a class does something wrong but doesn't own up? How do you feel if everyone is punished for something one person has done?

SO WHAT?

- How do you think Marcel felt about visiting the country he used to live in?
- Why is it important for farmers to consider their animals' well-being?
- Why do you think Mr Thorpe suggested that Jade-Marie could have a go with the wheelbarrow?

- When do you think it would be right for a group of children to take the consequences of a mistake, rather than an individual?
- Why might Mr Thorpe have been more positive about Marcel's admission than the boy expected?

PRAYER

When we let ourselves or others down,
give us the courage to admit it,
and when we have the opportunity to help others,
give us the wisdom to do the right thing.
Amen

Life's too short to hold grudges

> ### WHAT'S IT ABOUT?
>
> When Ellie gets away from problems at home for a week, will her behaviour change?

Ellie was pleased that Group Five had Nicky as their adult leader. She got on OK with her Year Six teacher, Mr Thorpe, and Mrs Denly was fine for a head teacher, but it was great to have someone new to work with, someone who didn't know what you were really like sometimes. She liked school and she was good at most things, but getting on with other children could be really hard. That was one of the reasons she'd wanted to come on the farm trip in the first place. It was a chance to get away from everything for a week, especially Mum's new boyfriend, Phil. So far, things had gone well and she wasn't homesick at all.

They'd spent the morning separating the big sheep from the lambs with Mr Turner's son Alan, ready for moving the ewes, as the mother sheep were called, further away from the farm to recover from suckling their offspring. Alan was going to move the ewes to a field down the road with his cattle trailer later on, leaving the lambs closer to home so that he could keep an eye on them. Ellie could still hear the deep voices of the mothers calling from the big shed they'd been kept in, and the higher-pitched, almost child-like replies of the lambs. She'd really enjoyed meeting Molly the border collie, who was stern with the sheep but much more friendly with Ellie and Kishon, who'd both had great fun stroking her head when she wasn't working to round up the sheep and lambs.

Just after lunch, Nicky had brought them up to the top of the house, to the workroom, where it was their turn to make a tile. A ceramic artist, whose name turned out to be Matt, was working with each group in turn for an hour during the day. Matt was tall, with long curly hair and an earring. As the group took their seats at the two polythene-covered tables, he quietly welcomed them to the session, giving them each a sticky white label and writing their names on them.

'You're going to make a tile each to celebrate coming to the farm. I'll get them baked in my kiln at home before you leave, then you can take them home with you as a memento on Friday.' His voice was very calming and he smiled a lot between phrases. Ellie noticed that he had some classical music playing quietly in the background, and she realised how relaxed she felt. Charlotte was sitting next to her, with Errol and Kishon sharing the other table in the room.

'I'm going to have a go as well,' Nicky said, full of her usual enthusiasm. 'What comes first, Matt?' she asked the artist.

'You've all got a piece of paper and a pencil on your table, as you've already discovered—some of you.' This was addressed to Errol, who'd started tapping his pencil to the music, and Charlotte, who'd begun rolling her piece of paper round her finger as she listened. 'This is for you to design your motif on. Does anyone know what a motif is?'

The room was quiet for a moment before Kishon raised his hand tentatively. 'Is it like a computer icon?'

'Sort of, yes,' came Matt's response. 'It's a simple image or symbol that will make the basis for your design. Tiles usually work best if you take a bold, fairly simple shape or outline as the central focus. Think of what you've done so far on the farm and try experimenting. I'll do one too so that you can see how I play around with ideas. You can use the whole piece of paper, then choose your favourite motif and start working on a smaller piece of paper to draw your final design.'

Ellie tried drawing a pig but got stuck until Nicky showed her a book on one of the shelves, which had a photograph of a sweet little pig looking over a wooden door, its trotters resting on the weathered wooden boards. Ellie noticed, while she was putting the book back on the shelf, that Charlotte had drawn a beautiful cockerel on her piece of paper.

'Can you do me one of those, please, Charlie?' she whispered in her most persuasive voice, but Matt looked up from his designs and said how important it was that they should all do their own work.

Ellie tried surrounding her pig with flowers, but somehow they came out all wrong. After 15 minutes she found herself looking at something that resembled a dog looking out of a weather map. Matt decided to walk around the room at this point, making observations and suggestions about everyone's work.

'That's lovely, Errol, although I think you can simplify it even more in your final design.' Errol beamed with pride over his sheepdog motif, surrounded by very neatly drawn sheep.

'I like your cow's face, Kishon, although I'm not sure that the little tails you've drawn round it will work very well on clay. You might want to think again about that.'

Kishon was quite pleased, although Ellie could tell that he was a bit upset about having to redo the tails.

'Ellie, I like your sheepdog, too, but I think there's probably too much detail in your weather symbols, if that's what they are.' Matt looked a bit puzzled, then tried smiling at Ellie encouragingly as he added, 'You've obviously tried really hard, though, so well done, Ellie.'

Then came Charlotte's turn. 'Oh, now that's fantastic,' enthused Matt, picking the paper up to study it more closely. 'You've captured the very essence of a cockerel here, and I love the bees you've used in the border.' Charlotte glowed at the comments and smiled briefly at Ellie, who tried to return the expression, without much success. Typical of a Year Five to be so good. Ellie looked again at her own efforts and noticed that they were slightly out of focus. She quickly wiped her eyes with her jumper sleeve before anyone noticed.

'Now it's time to draw your tile design on the small piece of paper, which is the same size as your tile,' explained Matt. Once they'd all done that, Matt gave them each a square of flat, moist, brown clay on a piece of cloth. He put a variety of plastic tools on each table and showed them on his own design how to etch into the surface of the clay. Once they'd done that, he produced three jars of different coloured glazes so that they could add colour to their tiles, even though they had no clue, just from looking at the liquids, what colour they would turn out to be.

'We would normally part-bake the tiles once before we add the glaze, and then fire them properly,' Matt told the children. 'But we should get some interesting effects doing it this way, and I don't have time to put them in the kiln twice this week.' They tidied everything away busily, putting their designs in the bin and wiping the polythene sheets down with a damp cloth. As they were about to leave the room, Charlotte suddenly said,

'Where's my tile gone?' She was standing at the back of the room, looking at the table and pointing. 'I just came for one last look and it's not there.'

Everyone gathered round to see for themselves and to make sure that Charlotte hadn't missed something. Sure enough, her cockerel tile was nowhere to be seen. Nicky organised a search of the room, giving each member of the group somewhere to look. Charlotte was crying softly as she looked and kept dabbing her eyes with a tissue, so she wasn't really much help. 'It must be in here somewhere because no one has left the room,' Nicky murmured, mostly to herself.

Ellie glanced briefly at her, noting the anxious look on the farm supervisor's face, and decided that the time was right to act. 'Has anyone checked the bin?' she said brightly as she hurried across to it from the bookshelves that had been allocated to her as a search area. She bent swiftly down and rummaged among the pieces of paper, triumphantly producing the tile, slightly bent in one corner but otherwise undamaged.

Nicky smiled with relief and took the tile from Ellie. Matt joined her to help pick off some pieces of pencil sharpenings that had become stuck to the wet glaze. 'No harm done,' he announced when he'd straightened out the corner and replaced the tile on the table with the others.

On their way back downstairs for lunch, it was Errol, Charlotte's classmate, who told her in a whisper what had really happened to her tile, and who it was who'd smuggled it into the bin while they were all tidying up. Charlotte had already had her suspicions but hadn't wanted to say anything. After all, her work hadn't been spoilt too badly.

After they'd had lunch, there were 15 minutes of free time, and some of the children gathered on the farmhouse lawn to play games while they waited for their next jobs. Charlotte noticed Ellie playing swingball on her own, so she picked up a racket and walked cautiously across to join her.

'Do you want a game?' she asked.

'Yeah, all right, Charlie,' replied the Year Six, moving the string back to the halfway point.

Charlotte took a deep breath before adding, 'I know about the tile, but it's OK.' At first she thought Ellie was going to deny it, but she could see the girl thinking twice.

They started the game, smashing the ball backwards and forwards at each other, before the older girl finally got the upper hand and won.

'Why are you being so nice about it?' asked Ellie, rewinding the string so that they could play again.

Charlotte paused for a moment before replying. 'Because life's too short to hold grudges!'

MENTAL SWITCH-ON

How do you feel when someone forgives you? How do you feel when you forgive someone else? What makes it hard to do that sometimes?

SO WHAT?

- Why might it be difficult for Ellie if her mum has a new boyfriend?
- Why couldn't Ellie return Charlotte's smile properly?
- What else could Ellie have done when the search for the tile failed?
- Why do you think Errol chose to tell only Charlotte what he had seen?
- Why do you think Ellie didn't understand Charlotte's reaction to what she had done?

PRAYER

Thank you for the choices life gives us,
thank you for the opportunities we have to make a new start,
and thank you for the peace and joy that the gift of forgiving can bring.
Amen

10

It's just something someone gave me

> **WHAT'S IT ABOUT?**
>
> How will Alexia cope with the challenge of strawberry picking?

On the second night of the visit, the children listened to another chapter of a story in the lounge, munched their way through a biscuit each, drank their hot chocolate or cold milk and headed for bed. The staff were confident that they would sleep better, and, indeed, things were much quieter than the night before. In one of the two Year Six girls' dormitories, Alexia, Zara and Ellie had quickly cleaned their teeth and jumped into bed. Ellie was soon breathing with the regular, steady rhythm that suggested she was sound asleep. Zara and Alexia were in bottom bunks next to each other and began one of the whispered conversations that they'd so looked forward to, after they'd both decided to come on the trip.

'I've got strawberry picking tomorrow, but I'm not very happy about it,' murmured Alexia.

'Why not?' wondered Zara, the surprise showing in her face, even with the dim light cast by her torch.

'Because I'm bound to end up taking some and getting into trouble like I always do.'

'Hang on, it's a while since you pinched anything,' Zara responded with conviction. Alexia was the sort of person who sprang to everyone's mind whenever anything went missing in class, simply because, so often in the past, things had turned up in her tray or her coat pocket or her PE bag. 'You can change, you know.'

'That's easier said than done,' Alexia whispered with a sigh.

Zara wasn't sure how to respond, so she lay on her back, looking at the bottom of the top mattress through the criss-crossed wires holding the sleeping Ellie above her. There must be a way she could help. After all, what was the point of being a best friend if you couldn't come up with something in a situation like this? She fell asleep trying desperately to think of a plan. Alexia was soon aware that both the others were well away, leaving her alone with her own thoughts about how she would cope with tomorrow's challenges.

When Zara came into the dining-room for breakfast after doing her early morning work, she spotted Alexia sitting gloomily at the end of one of the tables, on her own. She quickly collected her cereal and joined her friend, hardly able to contain her excitement.

'I've got an idea,' she hissed under her breath as she splashed milk over her Weetabix.

Alexia looked sideways at her, a glimmer of hope showing in her eyes. 'What is it?' She sounded almost desperate.

By way of reply, Zara carefully offered her closed hand to Alexia below the table top. The other girl responded by placing her open hand on her lap, so that Zara could drop something into it. When she was able to examine it, Alexia saw that it was a friendship bracelet, made out of several strands of red, orange and yellow thread.

'When did you make this?' she whispered, wondering when Zara could possibly have found the time to do it during her busy morning.

'After feeding the horses,' Zara told her. 'We finished a bit early, so I asked Miss Shabani if I could go up to the workroom to make something, and she said that was OK, as long as I let Mrs Denly know. Mrs Denly was in her room writing a postcard, so she said it was fine as long as I left the door open. I knew there was some thread and scissors in the cupboard from when we tidied up after tile-making yesterday.'

'You two are as thick as thieves,' commented Mr Thorpe as he walked by with his empty plate. 'Plotting something, are we?' He smiled and the girls exchanged a conspiratorial glance.

'Just talking about our morning,' explained Zara, concentrating on her now soggy Weetabix for a few minutes. Meanwhile, Alexia slipped the friendship bracelet on to her left wrist and tied it loosely, tucking it under her sweatshirt sleeve in case anyone else saw it and started asking questions. The girls took advantage of a swell in the dining-room noise level to resume their whispered conversation.

Zara spoke first. 'All you have to do if you feel the urge to take something is to touch the friendship bracelet instead, and remind yourself that I'm rooting for you. Then you can tell me about it when you see me.'

'I suppose it can't do any harm to try,' responded Alexia.

'I know you can do it,' added Zara finally, before picking up her empty bowl and heading off to the hatch for some toast.

✪

Mrs Kitchen led her group across the edge of the potato field and through the gate into the pick-your-own area, where the late varieties of strawberries were still cropping.

'This is a variety called Albion,' she announced confidently, having been told all about it by Nicky before they set off. 'It's a special strawberry for picking in the autumn, so there should be plenty for our dinner tonight.'

'Where is everyone?' asked Ashley, looking around the field of raspberry canes, berry bushes and strawberry plants. 'If it's pick-your-own, there should be people.'

'The field isn't open to the public today,' answered Mrs Kitchen, handing out blue plastic baskets to the four children and keeping one for herself. 'Now the most important thing is not to be greedy,' she said. 'So why don't you all try just one strawberry to see what they taste like, and then make sure you put the rest in your basket so that we have enough for everyone to have some for dinner.'

The children were all given a row and were asked to place just one wellie-covered foot carefully on to the straw that had been laid down on each side of the squat green plants. Alexia plonked her basket on the ground by her right foot and started to search each plant in turn for the large red berries. The first one she found, she popped into her mouth, and felt the sweet juice exploding over her tongue, with the delicious strawberry flavour hitting her taste buds a moment later. It was wonderful. The next plant had three ripe fruits on it, and one that she left because it was still white and green over most of its surface.

After about ten minutes of picking, Alexia straightened up and stretched her back, bracing herself with her hands just above her waist. She looked around to see where everyone else was, and found that she had got left behind a bit. Ashley was near Mrs Kitchen and seemed to be coping very well with the freedom of being in a field as big as two football pitches. She could see, even at this distance, that his basket was filling up quickly. Martin and Kaci, the two Year Fives, were standing talking, not quite as far away as Ashley, but they had also picked a lot of berries. Alexia looked down at her own basket and decided to be extra vigilant for the next few metres to see if she could fill it even more quickly.

It was at this point that a picture flashed into her mind. It was the image of an enormous, ripe strawberry being lifted into her mouth by her own fingers, and there was nothing to stop her. She glanced at Mrs Kitchen and the other children in turn, but nobody was looking. Now was her chance. After all, two strawberries eaten rather than one wasn't much of a difference, was it? She bent down over the plants again, checked once more, and then stopped. In reaching out her left hand for the biggest fruit she could see, she noticed the red, orange and yellow threads peeping out from under her sweatshirt sleeve. She suddenly remembered the conversation with Zara over breakfast and pulled her hand back with a jerk. How close she'd come to giving in to her craving to eat another strawberry. She didn't need it, she told herself, and, as she reached out again, this time to pick the strawberry and drop it into the basket, she allowed herself a small sense of achievement and a smile to go with it.

Within an hour, the group had picked six full baskets of strawberries between them. They carried them proudly back to the farmhouse and round to the back door, where Mrs Turner, the farmer's wife, took the bulging baskets from them with a broad grin.

'You have done well,' she said. 'There'll be plenty for everyone tonight and quite a few for me to make jam with as well. Why don't you choose one more each for your efforts?'

As Alexia picked out a plump red strawberry from the

basket in Mrs Turner's arms, she reflected on her afternoon's achievement. She had managed, more than once, to avoid pinching any of the fruit, even when she knew that no one was looking. It felt like a new start, and she pulled her sleeve back briefly to have another look at her friendship bracelet.

'What's that, then?' asked Mrs Turner, peering down at it and taking it between her finger and thumb. 'Isn't it pretty?'

'It's just something someone gave me!' replied Alexia quietly.

MENTAL SWITCH-ON

What does the word 'temptation' mean? What do you find tempting? What's your favourite fruit? How does it grow and where in the world does it come from?

SO WHAT?

- How does Alexia feel about herself when she talks about always getting into trouble?
- What makes some people take things that don't belong to them?
- When is it all right to tell a 'white lie' (such as the answer Zara gives to Mr Thorpe)?
- What examples can you think of when someone else has helped you to make the right choice?
- How much is Alexia's achievement down to Zara?

PRAYER

Help us to make the right choices,
to know when to tell the truth,
and to help others whenever we can.
Amen

11

I try to be helpful

WHAT'S IT ABOUT?

When Omar and Lara fall out with each other, Kirsty must decide what to do.

It started during lunch time. Kirsty didn't see what happened, but something had obviously occurred between Omar and Lara, two of the Year Fives. Since they were both in Mrs Denly's work group, she took them to one side in the dining-room and spoke to them. Without making it obvious, everyone was listening to what the head teacher said, and the gist of it seemed to be that everyone was tired, they were in a strange setting and tempers could easily flair.

'You both normally behave very well, so I hope this will be an end to it,' finished Mrs Denly, looking meaningfully into both children's eyes until they nodded their agreement and were prepared to shake hands as a sign that they were sorry.

Mrs Denly took Kirsty and the rest of her group over to the dairy to meet up with Mrs Turner in the afternoon. It was a cool, white-painted building next to the milking parlour, with a huge stainless steel tank standing at one end. The farmer's wife proceeded to explain a bit about milking. A series of pipes carried the milk all the way from the suction units, or clusters, hanging from the cows' udders into the steel tank, and a tanker lorry collected it each morning using a big flexible hose. The cows were milked twice a day, once between six and eight o'clock in the morning and again between four and six o'clock in the afternoon.

Mrs Turner lifted the tank lid to show them where the milk would go once the cows were milked later, and she pointed out the enormous paddle that kept the milk moving while it was being cooled down from the cows' body temperature.

'The tank is like a giant fridge,' she explained. 'Even when it's chilled, the milk is kept moving to stop the fat from rising to the top.'

'I know the cows are brown and white, but is there a name for the breed?' asked Kirsty.

'They're called Ayrshires, duck,' answered the farmer's wife. 'Has anyone else got any questions before we go down to the cheese-making area?' Sam put his hand up and, when Mrs Turner looked enquiringly at him, he said, 'How much milk does a cow produce in one day?'

'What a good question, Sam,' added Mrs Denly, looking pleased. 'I was wondering that myself.'

'Just after she's had her calf, an Ayrshire cow will produce about 50 litres a day.'

'Wow!' said Sam. 'That's 25 lemonade bottles full,' he observed immediately, demonstrating why he was in the top Year Six maths group with Kirsty.

Mrs Turner then showed the children the cheese-making section of the dairy. She explained that only a small amount of the milk that the farm's herd of 60 cows produced was used to make cheese, because everything was done by hand. She then showed them a long shallow stainless steel trough with a creamy solid in it. It looked to Kirsty a bit like the crème caramels that she always put in the supermarket trolley when her mum would let her.

'This is curd, everyone. I made it earlier this morning by heating some milk to pasteurise it, adding a starter culture of bacteria to it, then putting something called rennet into it to make it set. Do you know where rennet comes from?'

The children looked at each other and then at Mrs Denly, who had the satisfied look of someone who knows the answer.

'Who would drink the milk if the farmer didn't take it out of the cows?' Mrs Denly prompted, looking around at the puzzled faces.

'The calves,' said Omar, although, from the expression on his face, it was clear that he couldn't see where this was leading.

'And where would the milk go first after they'd drunk it?' went on the head teacher.

'Into their stomachs,' answered Lara, looking immediately at Omar, who was next to her. Kirsty noticed that there was still some tension between the two younger children, although Mrs Denly was so interested in the cheese-making discussion that she didn't seem to be aware that there was still a problem.

'Exactly,' replied Mrs Turner. 'And you get rennet from ground-up calves' stomachs—although we use a vegetarian rennet that comes from plants, so that people who don't eat meat can still buy our cheese.'

Next she took a knife from the worktop and started cutting the curd into chunks, making sweeps with the blade in straight lines going both ways so that the curd was soon chopped up into lots of large cubes, still standing in the trough. Kirsty noticed that juice was appearing between the cubes, and she asked what it was.

'That's whey,' Mrs Turner told her. 'It's mostly the water from the milk, but there's some goodness in it so we give it to the pigs.' She went on to open a tap at one end of the trough so that some of the whey could drain into a bucket that was standing ready to collect it. 'We'll have to strain the rest out later,' she explained, 'but now we're going to chop the curd up into smaller pieces, and that's where you come in. Two of you can scoop the curd out into a bowl and two of you can put it through the curd mill here.'

She showed them yet another piece of equipment, which fitted over the trough on two pieces of wood at one end of the trough. It looked very old, possibly Victorian, and it had a short wooden handle which turned two rollers with teeth on them. Kirsty saw a chance to keep the two Year Fives apart for a while, so she spoke to Mrs Denly.

'Why don't Omar and I get the curd out of the trough, then Sam and Lara can put it through the mill.'

Mrs Denly smiled and nodded. 'That's a great idea, Kirsty. But first, I think we should all wash our hands again, don't you think, Mrs Turner?'

The farmer's wife nodded vigorously and handed them an anti-bacterial wash dispenser, like the ones Kirsty had seen at her doctor's. Once that had been passed round, and their sleeves were rolled up, the group got started.

Omar used a large plastic spoon to fill the stainless steel bowl that Kirsty was holding, beginning at the end where the mill was standing. Then Kirsty passed the bowl carefully to Sam, who gradually tipped the large chunks of curd into the top of the machine. When Lara turned the handle, the curd was squeezed between the two rollers and came out in much smaller, even-sized cubes. It fell back into the trough in a creamy-coloured cascade, where it started to make a pile. The children could see the rest of the whey beginning to trickle down the floor of the trough towards the tap.

'You keep busy with that while I go and sort out the moulds with Mrs Denly,' suggested Mrs Turner. 'We're just over there by the sink if you need us,' she added.

As soon as she'd gone, Kirsty asked Omar what had happened earlier.

'Lara was winding me up, calling me names, so I hit her— not hard. My dad says I should stand up for myself when people are rude to me.'

'Why was she calling you names?' continued Kirsty, passing the bowl to Sam again so that he and Lara could repeat their part of the process. As she turned the handle, Lara joined in.

'He wouldn't pass me the tomato ketchup. He kept moving it just out of reach and saying I was just a silly girl with short arms. So I told him he was stupid.'

'You said I was a stupid... I don't want to say the word. It's racist,' Omar responded, forcefully.

Kirsty looked at Lara, who couldn't meet her gaze. As Sam passed the bowl back to her, Kirsty asked him what he thought.

'I'm keeping out of it,' he answered. 'It's got nothing to do with me.'

'Well, I think you're both nice people but it seems to me you're both at fault,' Kirsty pronounced, 'and if you're going to enjoy the rest of your time at the farm, not to mention the rest of your time at school together, then you'll have to get over it.'

'She's right,' said Sam in the silence that followed, clearly deciding that it would do no harm to back up what had been said.

Omar seemed suddenly relieved about something, at exactly the same time as Lara relaxed, too. They looked at each other with the briefest of smiles.

'Why don't you swap with Sam, Omar?' suggested Kirsty, seizing the moment. 'Then you could work the mill with Lara.'

Omar hesitated for a second before nodding and slowly exchanging places with the Year Six boy. Kirsty took the plastic spoon, filled the bowl in Sam's arms and sighed with satisfaction. It was too soon to be sure, but they seemed to be on the road to recovery.

The two adults returned with some round moulds lined with thin cloth. Kirsty supposed that they were now going to put the curd into the moulds, ready for the next part of the cheese-making process.

'You've been very busy,' observed Mrs Denly, 'especially you, Kirsty.' The head teacher's eyes twinkled as she held Kirsty's gaze for a while. She must have heard us talking, thought Kirsty with a warm glow.

'I try to be helpful!' she said, pushing her plastic spoon deep into the curd.

MENTAL SWITCH-ON

How does it feel when someone calls you names? What difference does it make if an insult is true? What is racism? Why is it wrong?

SO WHAT?

- How else might children show that they're sorry, apart from shaking hands?
- Why do you think Lara looked immediately at Omar when she'd answered Mrs Denly's question about milk?
- When is it all right to get involved in someone else's problems and when does it become interference?
- What happened while they were making cheese to help Omar to move on?
- When have you felt satisfied lately with something you've done?

PRAYER

May the words that we use
make others feel good about themselves
and bring peace where there is trouble.
Amen

12

You never see anything like this at home

> **WHAT'S IT ABOUT?**
>
> It's the turn of Jon and the rest of his work group to look around the farm at night.

As they were all sitting enjoying their dinner on the third day of the trip to Vicarwood Farm, the children's conversation was halted by Tony, one of the farm supervisors, who raised his hand in the agreed way until everyone joined in and silence reigned.

'Can I remind Group Three that it's your turn to do the night-time look round this evening. You need to meet me in the barn at eight o'clock tonight, please, in your waterproofs in case it rains, because the forecast isn't great. That means that you'll be last in the showers and into your night gear, of course.'

The teaching assistant who led their group, Miss Shabani, looked carefully around the room at each of her team in turn to make sure they'd heard. Having assured herself that she wouldn't be on her own in the barn later, she returned to her mug of tea and her chat about the day so far with Mrs Kitchen, the other teaching assistant.

Jon resumed eating his apple pie and custard, reflecting also on the day's events. They'd had a good time feeding the horses and picking the horse muck out of the stables with enormous rubber gloves on. It had been a bit smelly, but the horses were such impressive animals that it was exciting just being around them. Yes, they were a bit scary because of their enormous size, but, in spite of their obvious power, they were very gentle. He'd never been so close to a horse before, except when two police horses and their riders had called into the school when he was in Year Three. Admittedly he'd been much smaller then, but he remembered being petrified by the huge, shaggy white hooves that had planted themselves on the playground, like the roots of enormous brown trees, and he'd kept himself safely at the back of the class while the children posed together near the horses for the photographer from the local paper. Now he felt much more confident, and would probably have had a go at riding one of the farm's four horses if Nicky hadn't told them that they weren't allowed to because of health and safety.

They'd picked pears in the orchard during the afternoon, walking beside the trees that were trained along the outside of the kitchen garden's brick walls, and even using short ladders to reach the higher fruit. Nobody had been stung, in spite of the number of wasps that had been buzzing threateningly around, looking for opportunities to get their own share of the harvest.

Jon had had the chance to get to know Andrew from Year Five pretty well over the last two days of farm activities, and had decided he was OK. Holly and Zara, who were in Year Six with Jon, had kept themselves to themselves pretty much, and that had suited him fine, but he would probably have been a bit lonely if Andrew hadn't been such a good laugh. Miss Shabani was cool, too. She reminded Jon of his Auntie Jayne, who was great fun, almost like a big sister, but who could be firm too when she needed to be. Taking everything into account, he was having a fabulous time.

Jon pulled the door to the drying-room closed after him and followed Miss Shabani and the rest of the group across the yard, playing the circular beam of his torch against their backs as he hurried across the cobbles to catch them up. They'd all put on their wellingtons again, as well as the bright yellow waterproofs that were almost regulation wear, but the sky was clear and they could see the moon to their left as they made their way to the barn doors. As Miss Shabani reached out for the latch, the most bloodcurdling screech reverberated around the farmyard. Everyone froze and the children looked at each other, holding their breath and feeling the tiny hairs on the backs of their necks prickling with a mixture of fear and excitement.

'What was that, Miss?' whispered Andrew, his eyes showing white and round against the surrounding darkness.

'I think it was a fox,' she answered.

'That's right,' answered Tony quietly, making everyone jump because they hadn't seen him coming up to the barn from the other side of the yard. 'It's a vixen, a female, calling out to her cubs. They'll be venturing further in search of a territory of their own and she's trying to keep in touch with them. Let's hope your friends shut the chickens up well this evening before they came in.'

He followed Miss Shabani into the barn, and the children joined them both inside, just as Tony found the light switch behind the door. As the bright light flooded the area, Jon spotted something dark and furry scurrying along the side of the wall nearest to him. Almost as soon as he saw it, the animal disappeared into a dark hole in the corner, leaving a long thin tail showing for a split second before that too vanished.

'I think I've just seen a rat,' he said.

'That's very likely,' responded Tony without any emotion. 'We keep plenty of cats on the farm and they will catch the young rats, but there are always some adults around. That's one of the reasons why it's so important to keep washing your hands before you go into the farmhouse. Rats carry one particularly nasty disease called Weil's Disease, which can be fatal sometimes.'

'Don't they like the light?' asked Holly, moving quickly behind Miss Shabani and looking around to make sure there were no more of the large rodents about.

'No, they're usually more scared of us than we are of them,' said Tony reassuringly. 'Sometimes they'll jump at a human when they're cornered but they usually keep out of our way.'

Jon was slightly reassured by this but he kept his eyes on the hole for a while, in case the rat came back. Tony explained what they were going to do. They had to look round the calf shed, the pig sty and the orchard to make sure that all the livestock were safe and happy, and they set off behind Tony in single file because he knew his way around. Before they left the barn, Tony flicked a big master switch down with a loud clunk, which made a dramatic difference to the farmyard when they went out. Now there were several floodlights casting vivid pools of clear white light around the yard. Moths and flies were suddenly visible, flitting in and out of the beams and gathering by the bulbs, attracted by the brilliance of the light.

They went to each of the sheds in turn, looking at the different groups of animals to make sure that none of them was distressed. Tony checked the water troughs, and the children simply walked along the passageways, leaning occasionally on a wall or a fence to observe. The calves turned their huge liquid eyes towards the group of humans but, sensing no danger, continued to lie or stand peacefully in the deep clean straw that had been spread that morning by the children now walking past it.

The pigs were sleepy but looked briefly at their visitors as they peered over the half doors, the children standing on tiptoe to see inside. Next was the orchard, where there wasn't a light, and everyone's torch became essential if they were to walk without tripping over food troughs, fallen branches or the pieces of machinery and implements that were stored there when not needed. They visited each chicken shed in turn to make sure that all the doors were fastened properly and everything was quiet.

When they reached the gate where they'd come in, Tony stopped them.

'I've got an idea, since conditions are about perfect tonight,' he said. 'When I say "now", I'd like you all to switch your torches off and find out what you can see, as well as what you can hear and smell and feel. Three... two... one... NOW!'

Jon couldn't believe the blackness that surrounded him. He could sense Andrew next to him and then became aware of his breathing. A cloud must have come across the moon because there wasn't any light at all. Jon heard one of the calves coughing, and an owl called from a large tree by the farmhouse. He could smell the grass at his feet and the sour scent of the chicken shed nearby.

'Now look up into the sky, everyone,' whispered Tony, and, as they did so, everyone gasped simultaneously. Above them were thousands upon thousands of stars, glittering and twinkling in competition with each other, so that Jon didn't know where to look. He had to speak, to share his feelings with someone, even though he really didn't want to break the spell. He settled for the tiniest whisper to Andrew at his side.

'You never see anything like this at home!'

MENTAL SWITCH-ON

How do you feel about going out at night? Have you ever been anywhere really dark? What can you remember about it?

SO WHAT?

- Apart from confidence, what else changes as you get older?
- When is it a good idea to look back on something you've done?
- When have you experienced the hairs on the back of your neck standing up?
- Why was the darkness so strange to Jon?
- Why did Jon feel under a spell, do you think?

PRAYER

When we experience new and amazing things,
when we wonder at the marvels of nature,
when we look up at the rest of the twinkling universe to which we belong,
help us to remember how tiny we are next to you.
Amen

13

I can't believe how quick you've been

> **WHAT'S IT ABOUT?**
>
> Harry really misses his games console when he has to hand it in at the farm for safe-keeping, but will he find a chance to use it in secret later?

It was the last full day of the farm visit, and Harry woke up raring to go. He hadn't been sure when they first arrived. It was so different from home, which was right in the middle of town, but he'd gradually got used to the quiet, the gentleness of the animals, and the beautiful landscape that was the fields, woods and hills. He was sleeping well at night in the dormitory, surrounded by the four other Year Five boys, especially Errol, who'd had been the first person to speak to him when he started at Winding Way Primary School last term.

Harry had moved up from the south of England, near London, and he'd quickly realised that his accent was very different from everyone else's. When Errol had approached him in the classroom on that first morning, he'd been worried that he was going to take the mickey out of the way he pronounced things, but instead the boy had offered to show him round school for the rest of the day. During a football game at playtime, he'd found out that Errol had only come to the school six months ago from Leeds, where he'd been born, and that he had a cousin who lived in London, so he was used to the different way that southerners pronounced their words. His grandad was from Jamaica originally, but he'd come over to Britain when he was a boy and had been here ever since. Everyone seemed to get on with Errol—it was something to do with his fantastic sense of humour, probably.

Errol had taken him along to football club on his first Friday, which was where he'd met a lot of the Year Six boys, and they seemed to accept him because he was pretty useful, especially in front of goal, where he often just seemed to leap to the right place at the right time.

As Harry walked down the farmhouse staircase with Errol to join Mr Thorpe, the Year Six teacher, and the rest of his work group, he suddenly remembered the two difficult parts of the trip so far. The first had been when he discovered that he wasn't allowed to keep his Nintendo DS or his mobile phone at the farm. Nicky, one of the farm supervisors, had told them that there were no computers or televisions here at all, and he hadn't known at the time how he was going to manage without them. Still, this was the fourth day and he hadn't really had time to think about them, if he was honest.

'What do you miss about home?' he asked Errol, casually.

'I miss my bedroom, and my computer, and my little brother,' replied his friend after a moment or two's thought. 'What about you?'

'Same really, except for the little bruvver bit, 'cos I 'aven't got one. Plus what wouldn't I give for a go on my DS?'

'I wonder where Mr Thorpe has put them all,' said Errol, thinking aloud. 'I bet they're in his room somewhere.'

The mention of Mr Thorpe reminded Harry of the

other unhappy episode of the visit so far. That had been an unfortunate incident on the second morning when the pigs escaped from their sty, possibly because Harry hadn't closed the door properly—he couldn't really remember. Mr Thorpe had been pretty upset about it until Marcel came forward and took the blame, but Harry couldn't help feeling bad about it still. He would probably have Mr Thorpe as his teacher next year, and he felt he'd got off on the wrong foot for sure.

Now that he'd had time to think about his games console, Harry found it hard to put it out of his mind. Even though the different lifestyle at the farm had its own attractions and advantages, he began to feel a real sense of loss as he walked into the drying-room to put on his outdoor clothes.

Group Four found themselves piling up straw bales after breakfast later that morning, in one of the fields that had been combined the day before. Wet weather in August had put the wheat harvest back quite a bit, and, now that the contractor's combine harvester had moved on to another farm, Alan, the farmer's son, had to drive up and down the rows of straw with his tractor, towing a baler—the machine that packed the straw into blocks and tied two strings round them. There was quite a bit of dust and noise, and an obvious danger that meant the children had to keep well out of the way. However, now that one side of the field was finished, they were allowed to work in it while Alan went back to the yard with his tractor to fetch the big round baler to finish the rest of the field.

The small bales had been dropped off in higgledy-piggledy groups of twelve by a steel sledge that was towed along behind the baler, but Alan needed them piling up into sixes, a bit like Lego bricks, so that another day he could pick them up with his tractor's fore-end loader and put them on a trailer to take them back to the stack yard. Once there, he and his dad could store them in the Dutch barn, where the corrugated steel roof would keep them dry for use as animal bedding throughout the winter.

Mr Thorpe and his group had been given thick leather gloves so that the straw didn't scratch their hands. The teacher was able to lift the bales on his own, using his knee to push them into place on the piles, but the children had to get hold of an end each so that they shared the weight. Alan had said that they could take off their waterproofs, as the straw was dry and there was very little chance of bacterial infection this far from the farmyard. It was a good job, thought Harry, because the sun was rising in the sky and it was hot work. He had been paired with Marcel because they were well matched for height, and they were getting on well. Marcel was competitive, and he was keeping score of how many piles the boys had made compared to the girls, as well as keeping a check on how much help Mr Thorpe was giving each pair. They walked with a crackling, swishing sound through the long stubble that had been left on the floor of the field by the combine, until they reached the next clump of bales. Then they went into action. Sometimes there would be an extra bale, which they would have to carry across to the next group, and it was while they were doing this that the teacher strode across to meet them.

'Harry, could you do me a favour, please?' he asked, wiping his forehead with his shirt sleeve to dry some of the sweat off it. 'I've come out without my camera, and I'd like to get some shots of what you're all up to. I can't leave you lot unsupervised in the field, and we're very close to the farmyard, so I thought you could go, Harry. It's in my bedroom.'

This was an opportunity, Harry thought, for him to prove himself to Mr Thorpe, so he leapt at the chance.

'Of course I'll go, sir,' he answered, full of enthusiasm.

Strangely enough, it wasn't until he was climbing the staircase that Harry remembered about the Nintendo and

Errol's theory about where it would be. He'd been so busy stacking bales that the sense of longing had temporarily disappeared, but as he turned the door handle and put his head into the teacher's bedroom, he was aware of his eyes searching every surface for the biscuit tin that they'd all seen their electrical gadgets disappearing into. He spotted the camera case almost immediately, on Mr Thorpe's bedside cabinet, and strode across to collect it, checking that the camera was actually inside. As he turned, he happened to look down at the floor and there, just visible under the bed, was the bright red biscuit tin. Here was his chance to have just a little go. No one would ever know that he'd done it—except him, of course.

Mr Thorpe and the rest of the group were sitting on three bales having a drink from their water bottles when Harry returned to the field. He galloped across the stubble, the camera case bumping against his hip, and gratefully took a slurp from his own bottle when he reached them.

'Good grief, Harry,' said Mr Thorpe, putting the lid back on his bottle. 'I can't believe how quick you've been!'

MENTAL SWITCH-ON

Which computer games do you like playing? How often do you play? What's the longest time you have ever gone without playing a computer game or watching TV?

SO WHAT?

- Why do you think Errol was so keen to help Harry settle in when he started at Winding Way Primary School?
- What do you think you would miss about home if you were staying on a farm?

- What does it tell you about Mr Thorpe when he chooses to send Harry to fetch the camera?
- Do you think Harry had a go on his Nintendo? What makes you think this?
- What does Mr Thorpe think about Harry after he has fetched the camera?

PRAYER

When we are tempted to make the wrong choice,
make us determined to do what's right,
and when our lives are crowded with things to do,
help us to find peace in simplicity.
Amen

14

I haven't felt this good in ages

> **WHAT'S IT ABOUT?**
>
> How will Charlotte and her work group cope with a repetitive and rather boring job in the barn?

When Nicky took her work group across to the barn after lunch on the fourth day of Winding Way Primary School's visit, she realised she was going to have problems. The children had been away from home for nearly a week now, and she recognised the telltale signs of tiredness and possibly even homesickness. Nicky had worked at the farm for just over two years and she loved it, even though the work got a bit repetitive at times. There were only so many ways that you could show a bunch of children how to clean out a pigsty or pick apples, but she never tired of seeing the difference in their faces from the time they arrived—excited yet uncertain—to when they left, tired but somehow happier with themselves.

Nicky had to admit that the job they had to do next wasn't the most interesting or rewarding one of the week, but it had to be done and she had to sell it to her gang.

'Gather round, you lot,' she said when they reached the

barn, trying hard to inject as much enthusiasm into her voice as she could. She was pleased to see that the two Year Five children, Charlotte and Errol, were the first to join her next to the enormous mountain of cattle feed. She couldn't help having a go at the two Year Sixes as they trailed in some way behind the others.

'I'm not very impressed by your attitude, Kishon. You're not setting a very good example this afternoon, I must say. And as for you, Ellie, you look as though you don't want to be here at all.'

Ellie muttered something but fortunately Nicky didn't quite catch it.

'Anyway, enough of me going on at you. Your job for about the next hour, all of you, is to tidy up this heap of cow cake ready for another delivery tomorrow. We've got to bag some of it up, and the whole barn needs a good tidy.'

She clapped her hands energetically but it didn't seem to have much of an effect on Ellie's level of enthusiasm. 'Let's get some extra gear on for health and safety,' she added, hoping that it would help the girl to snap out of it.

She handed out gloves and dust masks to them all, putting on the same things herself. 'There'll be quite a bit of dust,' she explained, her voice muffled so that they had to strain to understand her. 'You can take it in turns in your pairs with these lightweight aluminium shovels and sweeping brushes. Kishon, why don't you work with Charlotte, and you can work with Errol, Ellie.'

Nicky showed them how to push the pile of cow cake further into the corner, one of them throwing shovel loads further up the heap, and the other coming along behind with the sweeping brush.

Charlotte had the shovel first and went at the pile fiendishly, throwing the little brown cylinders of cake high into the air but not really watching where they were going. Kishon tapped her on the shoulder and said something that she couldn't make out.

She took her mask off for a moment and asked, 'What was that?'

He also lifted the white cover from his mouth and suggested, 'Why don't you slow down and aim more carefully?'

Perhaps he had a point. She was gasping for air a bit, probably because the mask made it a bit harder to breathe, and maybe her arms wouldn't ache so much if she worked more slowly. She nodded as they both put their masks back on, and started again. Out of the corner of her eye she noticed that Kishon was working his way along the dust and the few pieces of cake that she'd missed, swaying steadily with the brush as he moved the edge about 50 centimetres across the floor with each swish of his bristles. He looked as though he'd done this before, and, even though she couldn't see his mouth beneath its covering, she was sure he was smiling.

'Why don't you try the shovel, Kishon?' she shouted, tapping him on the shoulder for extra emphasis.

'Okay, Charlie,' came his muffled reply as they exchanged tools. She liked it when people used the short version of her name—well, most people. They returned to work and Charlotte soon found that she lost herself in what she was doing, although within about five minutes she felt exhausted again. She wondered whether they would ever finish the job as she leaned for a moment on her broom handle to survey the mountain of cake.

Nicky came over to Charlotte and Kishon, having noticed that one of them wasn't working.

'Charlie, can you give me a hand to bag some cake up now, please?' she asked, offering the girl her shovel. 'Ellie, why don't you come and help, too?'

That left the boys to finish the heap, which was now right in the corner of the barn, leaving floor space for the next delivery when the bulk lorry came. 'I'll hold this bag open while you fill it with your shovels from the edge of the heap.'

'Why are we putting it in sacks anyway, Nicky?' asked Charlotte.

'It's for the young heifers out in the field, where there isn't quite so much grass at this time of year,' answered the supervisor, pleased to be able to pass on another nugget of farming information.

'What's a heifer?' wondered Ellie. Nicky smiled to herself, pleased that the Year Six was finally showing some interest.

'It's the name we give to a cow from when she's born until the time she has a first calf of her own.'

The two girls took it in turns to shovel cake through the open neck of the bag, and when it was full they dragged it together across the floor to lean it against the wall. By the time they got back, Nicky was ready with another bag and the whole process started again.

'How many bags have we got to fill?' said Ellie, sounding as though she probably wouldn't like the answer.

'Only 20,' replied Nicky brightly through her mask, just loudly enough for the girls to hear her reply. Thinking back to how encouraging Kishon had been earlier, Charlotte decided to speak. 'If we get into a rhythm, the time will go more quickly and we'll get more done.'

Ellie seemed to hear it because she paused for a second or two, and, from the look in her eyes, she seemed to be thinking. When she took up shovelling once more, it seemed to Charlotte that she had a bit more purpose about her actions.

'You'll also enjoy it more,' added Nicky for good measure. Sure enough, it seemed like no time at all before the bags were finished, the boys had completed their job, including sweeping up where the girls had been filling the bags, and they were moving on to the tidying that Nicky had told them about.

'This should just take us about 20 minutes, and then I'll take you over to the play area, because I can't believe what a fabulous team I'm working with now.'

Charlotte glanced round at all the faces and noticed that the eyes above the masks all had the little crinkles in their corners that gave away the smiles of satisfaction that everyone was wearing, including herself.

This was where their thick rubber gloves came into their own, according to Nicky, because anything in the barn could have mouse or even rat urine on it, and they had to keep that off their hands.

There were paper sacks in various places, and Nicky pointed out the little black mouse droppings that scattered off them when the children picked them up. Charlotte noticed that one of the farm dogs, a cheerful-looking chocolate Labrador called Alfie, had wandered into the barn and was showing a great interest in their activities.

'He's looking for mice,' Nicky explained, 'He enjoys the sport of chasing them, although I'm not sure he'd know what to do if he caught one.'

Just as she finished speaking, a small dark shape shot along the wall from behind a wheelbarrow. It was moving so quickly that Charlotte couldn't focus on it, and Alfie, hurrying along behind, couldn't catch it before it disappeared through a gap in the bricks.

The children worked hard for another five minutes, tying the sacks up into bundles with the orange baler string that was also lying around in places, and hanging them from nails in the wall to keep the mice out of them. Kishon stopped occasionally to stroke or pat Alfie, but otherwise everyone kept very busy. They paced themselves now as well, not rushing and then resting, but keeping going steadily until the work was done, the floor was swept, and the time had come to head off to the play area. As the children dropped their masks into the bin and handed their gloves back to Nicky, she praised them all for their efforts. Charlotte turned to Kishon as they walked out of the barn and summed up her thoughts.

'I haven't felt this good in ages.'

MENTAL SWITCH-ON

What job do you find boring? How do you make yourself carry on doing it if you have to? When did you last feel really good about finishing something?

SO WHAT?

- How do you think Nicky chose the pairs when they started the job?
- What difference does it make when people use shorter versions of your name, or nicknames?
- What makes it hard to be encouraging sometimes?
- Which rewards work well at school for you when you've done well?
- Why do you think Charlotte feels so good when they've finished the activity?

PRAYER

When we face a challenge that seems hard or boring,
help us to understand the purpose well enough
to make us persevere to the end.
Amen

I thought you'd nicked it

> ### WHAT'S IT ABOUT?
>
> Errol receives an unexpected present, but will he get to keep it?

During tea on the last full day of the farm visit, Errol was sitting with Andrew, one of his mates from Year Five, chatting about the different afternoons they'd had. The pizza they were eating was fantastic, and all the better because they'd been working so hard. Errol's group had been tidying and sweeping the barn, and had all had an early shower to get the dust off before their evening meal. Andrew's group had been outside chopping thistles in the paddock with sharp spades and thick leather gloves, trying to get out some of the roots that the grass mower didn't touch. Andrew's back was aching with all the bending they'd had to do, but at least the weather had been perfect, with bright autumn sunshine and a delicious breeze to keep them cool.

Once they'd finished their pudding, a tangy blackberry-and-apple crumble with a large scoop of vanilla ice cream, the boys decided to get their farm diaries from their dormitory and go to the workroom before evening jobs. When they entered the room, they saw one of their teaching assistants sitting near the dormer window that looked out on the farmyard below. She was hunched over a piece of fabric and sewing into it with a bright yellow thread.

'What are you doing, Mrs Kitchen?' asked Andrew, walking over to have a closer look. She looked up from her sewing to see who had spoken, and then smiled with recognition. 'Hello, Andrew,' she said. 'It's called embroidery. I'm a textile artist in my spare time, and I thought I'd just catch up on a bit of work before we go out to our evening jobs. Would you like to see?'

Andrew nodded, so she showed him the rectangular piece of material, with oddments of other fabrics sewn to it, and then hundreds of stitches in different colours added to it to create a sort of picture. Errol joined his friend, peering over his shoulder, and felt that he recognised some of the colours from his time on the farm. There was the brown and white of the cows, the gold of the ripe wheat, the lush green of the grass and the grey of the farmyard.

'Have you done all that this week?' he asked, astonished.

'Yes, in the evenings and in a few minutes here and there, especially when my group have been doing their diary time.'

'Is it meant to be the farm?' wondered Andrew, not sure whether that was the right question to ask.

'Well, it's based on my experiences, yes, but I've tried to capture the feel of the place rather than just doing a picture of one thing.'

'I think it's ace,' said Errol with real feeling, and Mrs Kitchen, smiling broadly at his generous comment, carried on with her sewing. The two boys chose a table to sit at and put their diaries down, ready to complete their Thursday entries. Errol had come without a pen or pencil, but he noticed that Andrew had brought his Man United pencil case, so he asked if he could borrow something to write with. His friend dipped deep into the case and pulled out his hand, holding a beautiful silvery pen.

'Why don't you try this?' he said, offering it to Errol, who took it hesitantly.

'I can't use this—it's far too valuable. What a fantastic pen!'

'Go on, you're fine,' replied Andrew, getting out a biro for himself and beginning to write his own account of the day.

Errol carefully took off the lid and pushed it on to the top of the pen for safekeeping. It fitted very snugly into place, and he was ready to begin. He couldn't believe how smoothly the pen glided across the lined paper of his diary. He'd never experienced anything like it. It said on the lid clip that it was a Parker rollerball, and Errol thought he'd seen something like it in the local newsagents in a display case, but he'd never tried one before. The pens at school tended to splatter ink across the paper when they were new, and the felt-tipped nibs soon got squashed or dried out. But this pen took writing into a whole new league—something like the Premiership.

Errol began to write about everything he'd done that day, and soon heard himself giggling with joy as he watched his words emerging on to the paper in beautifully smooth black patterns. This was fantastic—quite simply the best writing he'd ever done.

Fifteen minutes or so later, Mr Thorpe put his head round the door and told the boys it was time for evening work groups.

'I think you'll need to round your bunch up too, Mrs Kitchen,' he added as an afterthought. 'How's the embroidery going?'

'Very well, thanks,' she said as she headed past the boys towards the door. 'What smashing writing, Errol,' she said as she glanced down at his diary. 'And you, of course, Andrew,' she went on, not wanting to leave him out. 'We'd better get a move on or we'll get left behind.'

As Errol went to give Andrew the pen back, having clicked the lid firmly back on to it, his friend put up his hand to stop him. Then, zipping up his pencil case, he said, 'You can keep it if you like.'

Errol couldn't believe his luck. What a fabulous present—one that he knew he couldn't afford from his pocket money—but he knew he should refuse really.

'I can't accept it, mate,' he replied, 'though it's really good of you to offer.'

'It's OK, Errol, I've got loads of pens, and what's one more to me?' said Andrew, sounding as though he really meant it. Errol wavered. His mum's face popped into his mind's eye with a frown on it, and he was nearly sure that she wouldn't approve, but he wanted the pen so much.

'Well, um, thanks,' was all he could think of to say. He looked once more at the stainless steel barrel of the pen, the sleek lines and gold-coloured clip, and then slipped it into his zipped trouser pocket for safekeeping.

Later that night, after another chapter of their storybook had been read by Mrs Denly in the lounge, in front of a roaring log fire because of the nip in the air that evening, the children were enjoying their supper of hot chocolate and biscuits. The Year Five boys were clustered on a large sofa, eyes beginning to droop with weariness and faces glowing with the sun and wind they'd been exposed to during another hardworking day, as well as the heat that was blazing through the glass front of the stove.

'Have you still got that pen?' asked Andrew in a whisper. By way of an answer, Errol reached into his pyjama pocket and produced the pen, flashing it quickly at Andrew so as not to draw too much attention to it. He was just returning it to its hiding place when he noticed a strange look on Andrew's face, something very close to disappointment, but he decided he must have imagined it and took another soothing sip from the mug in his hand.

Errol was busy cleaning his teeth at the handbasin in the shower room when he was suddenly aware of a presence behind him, so he spat out the minty water from his mouth and looked over his shoulder to see who had come in. It was Andrew, bringing his towel in to put on the radiator. Errol turned back to the mirror above the sink to check that his teeth were clean, and was surprised to see Andrew's reflection, looking deep in thought behind him.

'What's up, mate?' asked Errol. 'You seen a ghost or something?'

Andrew was clearly wrestling with something, and, when he finally spoke, Errol realised he had been half expecting it.

'There's a problem about the pen,' muttered Andrew, looking down at the tiled floor as he said it.

Errol's mouth was suddenly dry and he could feel his heart pounding in his chest. This was ridiculous. It was just a pen, for goodness' sake.

'What about it?'

Again Andrew seemed to be struggling for words, before eventually spitting it out.

'When I saw how much you liked it, I just wanted to be a good friend and give you a present you'd never forget. But I've been thinking about it, and my dad gave it to me for my birthday, and I think he'd go mad if he found out.'

Errol thought for what seemed like ages. He thought about how he could go to Mrs Denly and say that he'd accepted a present and that, rightfully, it should be his. He thought about how much he loved that pen and how he'd probably never have the money to buy one for himself. He thought about how his mum would have to scrimp and save to get him one, assuming she would ever think that a pen was worth so much. But when he thought about Andrew's face, Errol reached into his pyjama pocket and pulled out the pen, offering it back to his friend.

'You had me really worried there for a minute,' said Errol, smiling as sincerely as he could. 'I thought you'd nicked it.'

MENTAL SWITCH-ON

What's the best present you've ever received? What made it so special? How do presents show us that people think a lot of us?

SO WHAT?

- When have you praised a grown-up for something they've done?
- Why do people praise each other?
- Why did Errol think he should turn down the offer to keep the pen as a present?
- What do you think made Errol decide that he'd imagined the look on Andrew's face?
- Why did Errol smile as he handed back the pen?

PRAYER

When someone makes a promise they can't keep,
or regrets a gift they've given,
let us put their peace of mind
before our own disappointment.
Amen

16

It can be amazing, too

> **WHAT'S IT ABOUT?**
>
> What will happen when Tamzin witnesses one of the cows calving?

On the last night of the visit, it was Group Four's turn to do the night-time look round, so they donned their outdoor gear, collected their torches and headed out into the farmyard with Mr Thorpe to meet Alan, the farmer's 25-year-old son. He came through the hand-gate beside the farmhouse from the part of the house where the Turners lived, pulling his coat over the boiler suit and wellingtons that he usually wore, especially around the cows. He had his chocolate Labrador, Alfie, plodding obediently at the heels of his green wellies, and a huge lantern in his left hand, its beam spreading a wide circle of white light on the ground in front of him.

Tamzin, one of the Year Six girls, stroked Alfie on the top of his dark brown head and ruffled his ears playfully as he checked the four children out in turn.

It had been a difficult week for her in some ways, because it was the first time she'd come away from home since her mum had lost her fight with cancer almost a year before. Her dad had been worried about her coming so far, not sure that she'd cope, but she'd been so busy at times that she'd almost forgotten about the dull ache that she had carried around with her for what seemed like a lifetime. At least she had Holly on the trip with her, the friend who, more than anyone else, had helped her through the darkest periods of the last year. And although she was worried about her dad back at home, she was comforted by the thought that he had her big brother, Lewis, to keep him company.

Tamzin missed the special box that Mum had put together for them all before she left them, with objects she had chosen and letters she had written. Tamzin often took it down off the bookshelf when no one else was around. However, she had brought along the bracelet that Mum had bought for her that last Christmas, and, although she wasn't allowed to wear it during the day, she slipped it on in bed so that she could feel close to her mum again, and not quite so alone. She could also pray more easily with it on, using the same sort of words that her youth leader Karen did on Wednesday nights at the local church.

'We'll go and check the cows in the calving shed first,' explained Alan. 'I'll just have to put Alfie in the barn for a few minutes, because cows get very protective when they've just had a calf, and that can be very dangerous if there's a dog around. Their instincts take over, and they behave as though they've smelt a wolf, so if any of us gets in the way we could be trampled. They're not as frightened of us humans, though, so if we're gentle there isn't usually a problem, especially with Ayrshires.'

When they arrived at the calving shed, Alan flicked on the light switch, climbed into the trough that hung on the barrier along the front, and then leapt expertly on to the clean straw below. There were three cows in the shed, two of which were lying contentedly chewing the cud and blinking at the light that now flooded their shed. The other cow was standing apart, near the far wall of the shed, her back slightly arched and a concentrated look on her face. She groaned quietly to herself as Alan approached her and then turned to look at him, unsure whether to move away or stand still. The young farmer's soothing words seemed to make up her mind for her, because she waited for him to pat her gently on the top of her head and rub her ear before running his hand down her neck and back as far as the top of her tail.

'Now, young lady,' he murmured, just loudly enough for the children to hear from their vantage point on the other side of the barrier. 'Have you started?'

As he said this, the cow spun round so that she was facing the wooden boards at the back of the shed, and Tamzin was able to catch sight of a small pink-and-brown muzzle protruding from beneath her tail. There also seemed to be a tongue just visible, poking through the slimy film that covered the mouth.

'I can see the calf,' she said to Jade-Marie, who seemed to be so captivated by the sight that she was lost for words. They had talked one lunch-time about Jade-Marie being a vegetarian, but she was clearly fascinated by the events unfolding before her, whatever she thought about eating meat.

'I think we're going to see it arriving,' she replied eventually, still not taking her eyes off the strange sight. Looking to her left, Tamzin noticed that the boys were spellbound too, as was Mr Thorpe, his mouth slightly open with concentration. Meanwhile, Alan had slowly moved his hands down from the top of the cow's tail to the calf's muzzle, and he pinched the tongue gently, noting with pleasure the way that it twitched.

'It's very much alive,' he reassured everyone as he marched back through the straw towards them, 'but we need to get it out quickly because I think she's been trying for a while.

There's a toolbox in the trough over there. Could one of you fetch it, please, while I take my coat off?'

Jade-Marie was the first to move and she soon returned with the brown-and-cream plastic box in her arms. She put it carefully in the trough so that Alan could lift it through the bars and on to the floor. He folded the top part back to show compartments inside, one of which held some blue nylon ropes. From the bottom of the box he produced two short lengths of polished broom handle before heading back across the shed to the calving cow. Halfway there, he turned briefly back to his audience to explain what was happening.

'When they're born, calves should come out with their nose between their front legs, a bit like you when you dive into water. Unfortunately, this one's got both its front legs back along its sides, so I've got to sort it out before it can be born.'

The cow suddenly lay down on the straw, and this time it strained very hard. Tamzin really felt for it as it groaned loudly, but the little muzzle still didn't move. Alan crouched down on the shed floor, rolled his boiler suit and shirt sleeves up to his shoulder, and squirted some antiseptic gel on to his hand and arm. He then slipped his hand carefully past the calf's nose and mouth until he was up to his elbow inside the cow. She stirred slightly, looked back down her flank and then strained again.

'Steady, girl,' said Alan. 'Not yet.'

He turned back towards the trough and called to Mr Thorpe. 'Would you mind giving me a hand, please?'

Mr Thorpe climbed carefully over the barrier and joined Alan, who had now taken one of the ropes in his hand. 'I'm going to tie this on to the calf's foot,' he said, 'and when I push the head backwards I'd like you to pull on the rope, which you can wrap round this piece of broomstick. That'll be a start, I think.'

When he got the word, Mr Thorpe pulled as hard as he could. As the muzzle disappeared, a small white foot took its place under the cow's tail. Then they had to repeat the process with the other foot before things could take their course.

From her viewing point, now standing inside the trough with the rest of the group, it all seemed to happen in quite a rush to Tamzin. One minute the two men were pulling, one on each rope, with the cow pushing for all she was worth, and the next minute a steaming, wriggling, spluttering wet calf was lying on the straw in front of them. The cow quickly stood up and turned round to start licking her new baby with a huge, rasping tongue. Within ten minutes the calf was nearly dry and was taking a few wobbly steps. Alan patiently helped the calf to find the teat that would give it its first few gulps of milk, and, with soothing murmurs from its mother, it began to suck. All was finally well.

'It's a heifer—a little girl,' Alan told them as he climbed back over the barrier with the bottle of gel and all of his equipment. Mr Thorpe looked very pleased with his efforts.

'That's a first for me,' he told the children. 'I've seen it on TV, but nothing prepares you for the real thing.'

As Tamzin watched the mother and daughter bonding together, she wasn't surprised to feel tears running warmly down her cheeks. From what she'd learnt that week, she knew that within a few days this calf would be taken away from its mum so that she could be milked by Alan twice a day, and the calf would have to cope without her. It didn't seem fair really, but then life wasn't always fair. One thing she did know, though, as she turned reluctantly away towards the barn and heard herself say it aloud to no one in particular: 'It can be amazing, too.'

MENTAL SWITCH-ON

What is a baby cow called? How do all mammals feed their babies after they're born? Why do humans drink cows' milk?

SO WHAT?

- What makes people pray?
- How should humans treat animals when they keep them as pets or on farms?
- How do you feel about eating meat?
- In what ways is life unfair sometimes?
- What have you found amazing about life?

PRAYER

Thank you for the marvel of life
and the amazing way it begins;
but help us to cope with the pain and sadness of its ending
and the mystery of what lies beyond.
Amen

It was nothing

> **WHAT'S IT ABOUT?**
>
> How will Kishon and the rest of his group use a few minutes of exploring time before breakfast on the last day of the trip?

It was the last morning of the farm visit, and the children had one more work session to complete before breakfast. They had tidied their rooms and packed their cases before getting into their waterproof gear because it was drizzling out on the farm. They'd been very lucky with the weather so far, Kishon thought, so they couldn't really complain. It was quite refreshing in a way to feel the light rain on his face as he set off with the rest of his group to fetch the cows in for milking. They were in the furthest field from the farm, according to Nicky, their supervisor, so the children had to get their skates on.

Kishon loved the Derbyshire countryside. He enjoyed the way the hills looked against the sky, and he liked the dry stone walls that lined the roads and some of the fields surrounding the farm. Even though they had to walk everywhere, so as not to frighten the pigs, sheep and cows, he still found it refreshing to be outside for so much of the time. Home was a bit cramped, if he was honest, with five of them in a fairly small flat over the newsagent's shop that his dad ran, and school was a bit noisy sometimes. But here, in the middle of nowhere, there was so much room. In some ways it was like Sri Lanka, where his grandparents still lived—but not as hot, of course. He'd only visited them once, but he remembered the heat as well as the sticky, warm air. England was so much fresher, like today with the showery rain drifting across the view and running in tiny streams down the front of his yellow waterproof coat.

When they came to the gate of the field that the cows were in, the brown-and-white animals were gathered together, waiting to be let through. Kishon was given the task of lifting the thick steel hook out of the staple in which it was resting, so that the gate could be swung towards them. As soon as it started to move, the cows pressed forward, their horny hooves scrabbling against the stones of the track beneath them as they walked patiently but purposefully towards the farmyard, where their burden of milk would be removed from their bulging udders by the milking machines in the parlour. Kishon and Ellie, as the two Year Sixes, had been given metre-long pieces of black plastic water pipe to use as sticks if any of the cows slowed down too much. A gentle tap or a prod on their rumps would keep them moving, but would also keep the children far enough away from the back of the cow to protect them from a cantankerous kick, should any of the cows choose to send one their way. The two Year Fives closed the gate behind them, because the cows were going somewhere different after milking, and then hurried to catch up with the herd as it made its way back to the farmyard.

Once the cows were safely fastened in the collecting yard and the plastic sticks had been put back in the barn, Nicky turned to the children and explained that they had some free time.

'It's your last day, so you can do some exploring, but there are some very clear safety rules. What do you think they are?'

'Have we got to stick together?' asked Charlotte hesitantly.

'That's right. Well done, Charlie,' replied Nicky, full of praise for the Year Five girl, who had really come out of herself as the week had gone on.

'And I suppose we have to keep out of any sheds,' added Errol, clearly hoping for approval from the group's adult leader.

'Absolutely,' replied Nicky, 'especially when there are animals in them. Anything else, anyone?'

The children thought long and hard before Kishon come up with his suggestion.

'I bet we have to keep within sight of the farmyard,' he said, not sure what difference it would make but feeling pretty sure that it would help somehow.

'Yes, sort of,' said their supervisor, thinking about how to put it into words. 'You can look around the yard, the orchard and the paddock. They are all near enough for two of you to fetch help quickly if you need it, and I'll be around doing a few bits of my own so that I can keep an eye on you. It's only 15 minutes till breakfast, so not a lot can go wrong. Just keep your ears open for tractors and be sensible about what you're doing.'

As the children headed off into the paddock, their agreed first choice for exploration, Kishon thought about the responsibility they had. This was the first time they'd been out of Nicky's sight for four days, and it felt slightly scary. What if something happened to one of them? Within a few minutes, however, he felt much more comfortable about it. This wasn't something he could ever have done at home. His mum and dad would have worried about him just being outside, even with three friends. They didn't let him play out at all really, unless they went to the park with him, and who wanted that in Year Six?

'There are some very funny people about,' his mum always said to him and, of course, they'd had the 'Stranger Danger' talks at school from the Community Support Officers. But here he was, in the middle of the countryside, going where he liked and doing whatever he wanted. To make things even more perfect, it had stopped raining and the sun was peeping through the broken clouds, bringing with it the first few patches of bright blue sky. He gazed at the newly weaned lambs that were grazing busily in small groups at the far side of the paddock, bleating occasionally to each other.

As Kishon walked through the long grass of the paddock, a bird suddenly clattered into flight from right at his feet, its long colourful tail trailing behind it and its alarm call echoing around in the cool damp morning air. He could feel his heart drumming in his chest with a mixture of excitement and fear.

'Don't worry, it's just a pheasant,' explained Ellie knowledgeably. She didn't normally speak to Kishon, even though they were in the same class, so he felt strangely pleased about it.

When they reached the hedgerow furthest from the farm, they stopped to take stock and decide what to do next.

It was Errol who first noticed the hole in the fence. There was a short piece of fencing in the hedge, where it was growing thinly, and there were two rails and a post fitted into the gap. Well, there would have been if one of the rails hadn't fallen off. This left a hole big enough for someone to squeeze through into the next field, if they were slim. Before anyone could say anything, Kishon had dropped to the ground and slipped his head and shoulders through, quickly followed by the rest of his body, squirming through in a commando crawl. Charlotte knelt down to see if she could see him, but there was no sign at all. Ellie called to him through the thick hedge.

'Are you all right, Kish?'

At first there was no reply, but then they heard a voice, strong and yet concerned at the same time.

'There's something wrong here,' he called. 'I think someone should fetch Nicky.'

'What is it?' demanded Charlotte, suddenly worried by his tone.

'One of the lambs is in here, but it's lying on its back and it looks very strange.'

'Is it dead?' asked Errol, kneeling down to see if he could get a view for himself.

Ellie and Charlotte decided to go back to the farmyard for Nicky while the boys stayed at the gap, one either side to stop any more lambs from getting through. It wasn't long before Nicky and the girls joined them again, all three of them out of breath from running. The boys learned that Mr Turner had taken his Land Rover the long way round into the other field, where Kishon was waiting with the lamb.

'It's making gurgling noises,' Kishon said eventually, 'so it can't be dead yet, can it?'

They all heard the sound of the Land Rover approaching the gap from the other side, and the door slamming as the farmer got out. They could only hope that he had arrived in time.

It wasn't until they were eating their breakfast that Nicky was able to clear up the mystery. The lamb had escaped into a field of clover which was meant for the cows to graze a strip at a time, controlled by an electric fence. It had eaten too much and the gas in its second stomach had blown the lamb up in an illness called bloat. Fortunately, Mr Turner had been able to release the trapped gas with a rubber tube passed down the animal's throat, and it was recovering well.

'So, in spite of breaking the rules, you're a hero, Kish,' observed Errol, after carefully swallowing a mouthful of toast.

'It was nothing,' replied Kishon, though his face showed that he clearly thought otherwise.

MENTAL SWITCH-ON

How does it feel when there are no adults around? What do you like doing and where do you like going when you're allowed to have some freedom? What are the dangers of being unsupervised?

SO WHAT?

- What is so special about being outside?
- What do you think Kishon's mum and dad imagine could happen to him if he played outside?
- Why was Kishon pleased by Ellie's comment?
- What made Kishon decide to go through the gap in the hedge?
- How do you imagine Kishon's face looked when Errol called him a hero?

PRAYER

Help us to enjoy the freedom we are given
and to use it wisely in learning more
about the world in which we live.
Amen

18

I'm good, thanks

> ### WHAT'S IT ABOUT?
>
> Jade-Marie reflects on her personality and begins to think that perhaps there are things she could change.

For the last time, Jade-Marie peeled her waterproof trousers off and hung them on the peg in the drying-room, underneath the matching yellow coat that she'd put there just moments before. She looked across at Kirsty, her best friend, and smiled with sheer delight. It had been a fabulous week. She hadn't used her inhaler once, she'd been busy experiencing and seeing lots of new things, and she felt really good inside. It could be her imagination but she was sure that she was getting on better with people. Not just her friend Kirsty. That was easy most of the time, probably because Kirsty usually went along with what she wanted to do—apart from being a vegetarian, where it was obvious from the meals they'd shared at the farm that Kirsty was as keen on meat as ever, especially the sausages that had been on offer most mornings.

When she thought about it, Jade-Marie had been quite impressed with what she'd seen at the farm, and if it wasn't for the fact that she didn't really like the taste of meat, she might have been persuaded to start eating it again by what she'd seen. The animals seemed contented enough most of the time, and the farmer and his family spent a lot of time making things comfortable for them and caring for them generally. Still, she couldn't believe that all farms were like this. She'd seen some shocking things on the telly, and in the end the animals would have to be killed if someone was going to eat them, and that was still the bit that upset her most.

Kirsty joined her as they walked into the dining-room for breakfast and queued up for their cereal and orange juice. This was something they'd both decided to keep doing when they got back home.

'I can't believe how much better I've felt in the mornings for having breakfast,' said Kirsty.

'Yes, but as I said last night in bed, will you be able to get up this early in the morning on a normal school day?' asked Jade-Marie.

Kirsty's face showed that she was far from convinced that she would, and they sat down in silence to ponder the question together.

Jade-Marie soon found herself thinking about other aspects of everyday life. She pictured mornings at home as they usually were, with her mum shouting up the stairs for the umpteenth time, 'Will you get up, Jade-Marie, you're going to be late for school!' She would drag herself out of bed and find that Michael, her older brother, was in the bathroom so she wouldn't be able to get near the shower. Then, when she went downstairs in her dressing gown to get a drink and a piece of toast and jam, her baby sister, Kylie, would be driving Mum nuts, banging her drinking cup and chucking half-chewed bread and marmite on the floor.

'Just sort out your sister, will you, while I do the pack-ups.'

It all seemed a million miles away from here, but perhaps, if she went back with a new resolve, things could be different. If she got up even half an hour earlier, she could easily beat

Michael into the bathroom and be ready for school in time to offer to feed Kylie for her mum. How good would that be?

The larger group of four Year Six girls who had shared a dormitory during the trip had to pack after breakfast. They had started out putting their dirty washing in their own black bags under the bottom bunks, but, by the fourth morning, things had got a bit mixed up. Because there were two bags under each bunk, it hadn't been too clear which one belonged to which girl, and when Jade-Marie tipped the contents out of hers, there were some items there that she didn't recognise.

'That's my T-shirt,' claimed Holly as Jade-Marie held it above her head. 'And those are my pyjama bottoms.'

'Why don't we tip everything out in the middle and pack our own stuff from the pile?' suggested Tamzin, who had found similar problems with her dirty washing. They agreed that the clothes in the chests of drawers, which hadn't been worn, could just go straight into their cases.

'I think it would be better if we took it in turns to hold up things that aren't ours, and it'll be less messy,' answered Jade-Marie.

'You always think your way's best, don't you?' burst out Holly from nowhere. There was an awkward silence as the girls thought about this, Jade-Marie included. Kirsty didn't leap to her friend's defence but just looked up from where she was kneeling by her case, rearranging its contents. The uncomfortable pause was ended by a strange thing happening.

'You're right, let's do it your way, Holly,' Jade-Marie heard herself say. She had no idea where that had come from, but she was surprised by how good it felt.

'Oh,' said Holly. 'That's settled, then.' She seemed equally baffled, but they soon had everything on the floor where they could all see it, and they were able to select their own stuff for packing in the tops of their cases, inside their individual black bags, in no time at all. Then Mrs Kitchen looked in to make sure that the room was nearly tidy and that the girls were almost ready to take their cases and rucksacks down to the hall.

'The coach will be here any minute and the driver will want to get on with putting the luggage in the boot as soon as he arrives. You look as though you've got everything under control.' She seemed suitably impressed, especially when she opened the shower room door and found that they'd remembered to clear all their washbags out.

When she'd gone, the girls looked at each other proudly, aware that they'd worked together well as a team.

'I don't mean to be bossy,' Jade-Marie said. 'It just comes across like that sometimes.'

Holly looked at her and smiled. 'Me, too, if I'm honest. I'm used to organising my little brother when he's getting ready for school and my dad isn't around because he's on nights. Sorry if I was a bit harsh just now.'

Jade-Marie realised that she wasn't alone in having responsibilities at home. That was another good thing about the farm visit—she'd really got to know some of her classmates like never before, and it helped her to understand why they behaved as they did sometimes.

They were soon dumping their cases by the front door in the long, cavernous hall of the farmhouse. It seemed longer than four days since they'd lugged those same bags up the stairs on arrival. It felt to Jade-Marie as if she'd been there for weeks. She did feel different, and that had been plain for all to see in the way she'd handled Holly's criticism in the dormitory. Perhaps I really have changed, she thought.

Once again, she thought about how things might be when she returned to school. She imagined walking into class, sitting down at the start of a literacy lesson and not putting her hand up when Mr Thorpe asked the first question. She pictured herself asking Mrs Denly if it was time for someone else to have a chance to work the digital projector in assembly. She considered not standing for School Council this year, and waiting to decide who she would support in the class election for a change. When she thought about all of this, it occurred to Jade-Marie that it wasn't just about her changing, but also about the opportunities it would give others to be different. As much as she was going to miss the farm, part of her was getting quite excited about going home.

Mr Thorpe supervised the carrying of luggage to the coach so that Mick, the same driver who'd brought them across to Derbyshire, could stow it easily in the luggage compartment. Ashley was being very helpful for a change, and Mr Thorpe noticed that Tamzin had really brightened up during the week. All in all, he thought, the visit had been a resounding success. If they could just get home safely and on time, he could really enjoy his weekend. One thing he noticed, though, was how quiet Jade-Marie was this morning. She looked happy enough, and he wasn't aware of any major upsets with other people, but she didn't seem her usual self. As she walked past with a tray of packed lunches in her arms from the farm kitchen, he stopped her and asked if she was OK.

'Mrs Denly says I've got to get a move on with these,' she told him before continuing on her way obediently. He tagged along with her, intrigued. OK, he'd only taught her for a couple of weeks, but he thought he knew her pretty well by now.

'I thought perhaps you were upset, or maybe even sulking about something.'

She stopped and looked at him, realising in that moment just how difficult it was going to be to reinvent herself. Still, she was determined.

'I'm good, thanks,' she said.

MENTAL SWITCH-ON

What do you most like about yourself? What would you like to change? Have you managed to change anything in the last year? Who has helped you to grow as a person in the past?

SO WHAT?

- How might Jade-Marie have come to the conclusion that she was getting on with people better?
- How do you feel about breakfast?
- How do you think imagining the future can change it?
- How well do you think your class teacher knows you?
- What could you do to change something about yourself in the next few weeks?

PRAYER

Help us to know and grow ourselves,
help us to imagine and dream for our future,
but above all help us to love ourselves as you love us.
Amen

19

I've got everything I want in here

> **WHAT'S IT ABOUT?**
>
> Will Lara manage to spend all her money in the farm shop before it's time for the coach to leave?

'Hurry up, children, we need to leave in the next ten minutes if we're going to be back at school by three o'clock.' Mrs Denly had the sort of voice that you couldn't ignore, but Lara tried hard to put it to the back of her mind as she attempted to focus on the decisions she had to make. She looked again at the £5 note in her hand before setting off once more along the shelves in the farm shop. She wanted to get a present for everyone in her family, but everything she looked at held so many memories of the fantastic week she'd spent at Vicarwood Farm, and she really couldn't decide what to get. The added complication of having to spend £5 or less was stretching her mental maths to the very limit, and the last thing she needed was to be told she had a deadline.

Kaci, her friend and fellow Year Five pupil, was just going over to the till where Mrs Turner, the farmer's wife, had been serving the groups of children for the last 20 minutes or so.

'Having trouble?' Kaci said with a knowing grin.

'Don't ask,' replied Lara. 'It's always the same with me.' At least she knew that about herself, but it didn't help right now. She took a deep breath. 'This is it,' she said, and reached out for her first choice.

She knew that her dad would enjoy a chunk of Derbyshire cheese as she lifted it down from one of the refrigerated shelves. This wasn't the exact cheese that Lara had helped to make, of course, but it was just like it, and at £1.50 it wouldn't make too much of a dent in her money. As she held the cheese in her hand, its feel brought back memories of the dairy, the cows and packing the curds into the moulds ready for pressing. Her dad would love it, even though she knew he would make apologetic speeches about his waistline to her mum while he was eating it. He usually claimed that he would burn off the calories at the gym next day, but everyone knew that the amount of time he spent there didn't come close to burning off half of what he ate that he shouldn't.

Martin walked past, making a strange growling noise. Lara looked to see if there was a reason, and spotted a cardboard and plastic box, so heavy that it took two hands to carry it, and Martin walking with it at eye level towards the till.

'What have you got there?' she asked. Martin stopped making the noise and came out of his daydream with a rather embarrassed look on his face. Rather than answering, he turned the box so that she could see into it through the clear plastic front. Inside was a model tractor, complete in every detail, and very much like the one on which she'd seen Alan, the farmer's son, roaring around the yard. She realised now that Martin had been imitating the tractor's engine noise as he walked through the shop, and she remembered him telling her earlier in the week that he was desperate to have a go at driving it.

'Did you get a go on Alan's tractor?' she asked.

Martin's face registered a flicker of disappointment now, but he quickly recovered his composure and replied, 'I'm not allowed to drive a real tractor till I'm 13, and then I'll have to be supervised by an adult. But I did get to sit on it one day without the engine running, when Alan wasn't busy. It was awesome.' His face took on another expression now as he clearly replayed the experience in his mind's eye. 'I'm gonna be a tractor driver one day,' he murmured to himself, as though saying it would make it more likely to happen.

'You'd better go and pay for that,' Lara prompted, seeing Mrs Denly heading back into the shop.

'Come on, everyone,' she said, 'Just another five minutes, please.'

Lara found herself in the pottery section a minute or so later, agonising over which mug to buy. They were incredibly cheap at only £2.50, being slight seconds, but she thought her mum would like one, especially when Lara told her that she'd met the man who'd made it. She thought about how much fun she'd had working with Matt, the ceramic artist, earlier in the week. She now had her own decorated tile stowed safely in the middle of her suitcase, folded carefully into one of her T-shirts for safekeeping, and it would be great to have another reminder of her time here. She chose a green mug with a duck's head design in relief on the side, and hung it from the fingers that held her dad's cheese as she moved on to the next section.

When she calculated how much money she had left, she was disappointed to realise that it was only a pound. That meant she could only afford one more thing, really, which she would have to give to her little sister, Amie. It wasn't a problem in itself, because she loved Amie to bits—well, most of the time, once she'd got used to the idea of having to share her mum and dad's time with someone else. Now Amie was three, she was a bit more fun, too, because she could actually do things rather than just lying there screaming as she'd done when she first arrived, or waddling into everything and being a nuisance, like when she was learning to walk. Now she was able to join in with a few simple games, and Lara had to admit that she was cute when she wanted a hug or listened to a story sitting on the sofa next to her.

As these thoughts were drifting through Lara's mind, her eyes lit upon a small stuffed pony, complete with felt saddle, bridle and reins. Lara reached down into the wicker basket to pick up the pony in her spare hand, and studied it carefully. As she did so, she remembered an incident earlier in the week.

They'd been mucking out the horses and ponies with Mr and Mrs Turner's daughter, Lucy, who was at university normally but hadn't gone back yet for the new term. Mrs Denly had gathered her group together when they'd finished their jobs and explained the situation to them.

'Group Two, you're very lucky,' she'd said, 'because Lucy has time to walk you all round the paddock on her old pony, Inca, if you'd like to have a go.' Omar had looked straight at Sam, his new friend, to see what he thought of the idea, and Sam had nodded his approval. Omar had surprised them all by going first, because he hadn't been very confident with the larger animals when he first arrived at the farm. They had all stood and watched as he tried on a small selection of hard hats to get the right fit, and put on the adjustable body protector, while Mrs Denly studied the risk assessments that hung in a dusty plastic folder just inside the tack room door. Mrs Denly had smiled her approval as she put the folder back, and Lucy had led Inca out of his stable on a short rope, with all his tack already in place.

First Omar, and then Sam, had levered themselves into the

saddle and made the short journey into the paddock and once round it, getting lost from view, before returning to dismount and let the next person have a go. Kirsty had been enthusiastic about riding, having done it once on holiday, and had taken her turn without a problem. But then everyone had turned to look at Lara, and she'd frozen, feeling her heart hammering in her chest and tears smarting in her eyes. She couldn't breathe and began to shake uncontrollably. It had taken a couple of minutes of Mrs Denly's gentle encouraging words to calm her down and enable her to place the foot of her wellington boot falteringly in the stirrup, allowing Mrs Denly to help her into the saddle. By the time they'd got half way round the paddock, Lara had begun to enjoy the experience of being rocked steadily from side to side on Inca's chestnut-brown back. She had felt her back and hips relaxing gradually, so that she felt a kind of oneness with the pony carrying her so effortlessly across the grass, which seemed such a long way below. This was something she'd have to try again, she'd decided as she jumped down on to the concrete stable yard with a mixture of relief and triumph.

'Are you having that, then, dear?' Mrs Turner's voice startled Lara back into the present, and she looked around to find her bearings. Of course, the shop, and the toy pony.

'Er… yes, please.' She followed Mrs Turner back to the counter, checking the price of the pony as she did so. Perfect—just a pound. And the tale she'd be able to tell Amie about her time riding would make it such good value for money, too.

'Aren't you getting anything for yourself?' asked Mrs Denly when Lara told her who was going to receive each of the presents.

'No, Mrs Denly,' Lara replied, smiling to herself and tapping the side of her head. 'I've got everything I want in here.'

MENTAL SWITCH-ON

What can you remember buying at museum shops when you've been on school visits? Do you try to buy something for yourself or for your family? Which are the best things to buy?

SO WHAT?

- How easy do you find buying presents for people?
- What have you dreamt of doing if you could?
- How might someone looking at you spot when you're frightened of doing something?
- What do you think Mrs Denly could have said to encourage Lara?
- What do you think Lara meant when she said she had everything she wanted?

PRAYER

Thank you for our families,
for those people who love us no matter what,
even though it doesn't always show in the way they treat us.
Amen

A lot can change in a week

> **WHAT'S IT ABOUT?**
>
> How will Andrew feel when he gets home?

Andrew handed his suitcase and rucksack to Mr Thorpe, the Year Six teacher, ready for them to be stowed in the boot of the coach that was ticking over with a gentle rumble in the farmyard. He walked quietly towards the door at the front of the coach, briefly catching a whiff of the rich exhaust fumes as he did so. The smell reminded him of so many great trips that he'd been on, but none compared even closely with the week he'd just spent at Vicarwood Farm. As he climbed the steps into the coach, he reflected on the last five days and found that he had mixed feelings about going home. He had got into the farm routine so completely—the early mornings, the late nights, the hard and varied work they'd had to do, the regular meals at a table in the dining-room—that he knew he was really going to miss it. However, he was looking forward to seeing his mum and dad again. His friends had been good fun and he'd made some new relationships, especially with Year Sixes like Jon, but the effort of getting on with people had been very tiring as the week had gone on.

When he reached the final step of the coach, Andrew noticed that the seat next to Jon was unoccupied and that Omar was busily chatting to Sam, another of the Year Sixes, as they shared a football magazine in the seat behind. This meant that he could join Jon, who looked up and smiled encouragingly as he lowered himself cautiously on to the half of the seat nearest to the aisle. Andrew put his carrier bag on the seat between them and rummaged inside for his games console. He was soon poised over the tiny screen, ready to attempt a new highest score on his favourite game, when Mr Thorpe called for quiet and asked all the children to face the front of the coach.

'Mrs Denly wants a few words, please, everyone,' he called out in a loud playground voice so that even Miss Shabani at the back could hear him easily. Mrs Denly climbed up the steps to take her place next to the driver, Mick, whom they all remembered so well from the journey to Derbyshire on Monday.

'I just want to say a big thank you to everyone at Vicarwood Farm for looking after us so well and giving us all a week that I'm sure we'll never ever forget,' she said, looking gratefully at Tony, Nicky and the Turner family, who were gathered by the open coach door, smiling up at her as she spoke.

'I think we should give them all a special Winding Way Primary School round of applause,' she added, raising her hands above her head so that the children and staff could see when to start clapping. They joined in with tremendous enthusiasm, so that wave upon wave of noise crashed around the inside of the coach before spilling out through the open door to those listening below. It was Nicky who responded to their applause by climbing energetically into the coach and thanking them for being such a good group, saying how much she and the rest of the team would miss them all.

As Nicky returned to the yard and Mick closed the door, the children waved and cheered through the windows at Mr and Mrs Turner and their son Alan, standing by the barn door with Tony and Nicky, the pupil supervisors. There were tears from some of the children, especially Ellie and Charlotte, who had caught sight of Alfie the chocolate Labrador wagging his tail and grinning hugely as the coach reversed towards the gateway on to the road. Before long they were speeding through the country lanes towards the motorway and the journey home. Andrew settled back into his seat, focused again on his games console and worked frantically away at the buttons with his thumbs, in search of that highest score.

After about two hours, the coach turned off the motorway and headed into the countryside again. Andrew and Jon knew this because they were both watching out of the windscreen just three seats in front of them, and sometimes gazing out of the large window on their right. They had put away their games, finding that the consoles had lost their appeal quite a bit during the week that they'd been shut away in Mr Thorpe's room for safe-keeping. The boys had also discovered that the view outside was much more interesting than it had seemed on the way to the farm, although they weren't sure why.

'I wonder what we're stopping for,' Jon said as they pulled into a car park with a large blue-and-white sign by the gate. The sign featured a black-and-white bird with a strange curved beak that turned up at the end. Black initials showed that it was owned by the RSPB, whoever they were.

Mrs Denly stood up as the coach stopped with a hiss of its air brakes, and she turned to face the back. 'We're having our picnic here at a bird reserve,' she announced. 'Does anyone know who it belongs to?' she asked, glancing meaningfully at the sign, which was clearly visible through the windows.

Andrew put his hand up and ventured an answer. 'Is it the Royal Society for the Prevention of... er... Birds, Miss?'

As soon as he'd said it, he realised it didn't make sense, and he could hear quite a few giggles from further back in the coach.

'You're very close,' replied Mrs Denly, smiling with amusement herself when the laughter had died down. 'See if you can find the correct answer while you're going to the toilets and looking at the visitor centre, everyone,' she added, pulling her fleece on and climbing down into the stone-covered car park.

Everyone filed into the visitor centre, used the toilets in turn, and then streamed chattering over to a group of six picnic tables that stood invitingly on a piece of carefully mown grass. They were about 20 metres from a lake, which was surrounded by tall straw-coloured reeds, whispering harshly to each other in the strong warm breeze. As Andrew gazed out on to the surface of the lake, he saw a large brown bird silently skim the tops of the reeds, lazily flapping its black-tipped wings and looking piercingly from side to side as it did so. He noticed that the bird's yellow feet had threatening talons at the ends of the toes, and that its short powerful beak ended with a sharp curved point. This made it a bird of prey, he suspected, which explained why the smaller birds in the reeds, and on the bird table near the picnic site, were darting swiftly for cover in what he now knew to be a hawthorn bush. He had seen plenty of those at the farm, and knew how much protection they offered, having accidentally scratched himself on their thorns more than once this week.

As suddenly as the bird had appeared, it was gone, and he turned his attention back to the sandwiches and crisps he'd been given by Mrs Kitchen, determined to look at the bird book he thought he'd got somewhere in his bedroom, when he got home later that afternoon.

The coach crested the hill on the dual carriageway and Andrew was able to see most of his home town spread before him through the windscreen, the six towering blocks of flats near his house clearly visible near the football stadium floodlights. He hadn't been away very many times, but this view always gave his heart a lift. In no time, they were pulling into the street outside Winding Way Primary School. There was the deputy head teacher, Mr Piper, waiting to greet them, standing by the gate among a group of parents who were trying really hard, Andrew thought, to look laid-back about their children's return. He watched from the top of the coach steps as Omar walked purposefully across to his dad, his head held high with pride in his newfound confidence. Andrew knew how worried Omar had been about going away, and he was thrilled by the change in his friend.

He also spotted Ashley, the boy who almost didn't make it on to the trip because of his behaviour, standing calmly with Mrs Denly while she talked with his mum. They were both smiling and Ashley looked very pleased with himself, so much so that Andrew almost didn't recognise him.

Finally, he scanned the adult faces until he spotted his own mum and dad, near the back, their eyes moving to and fro in an effort to locate him. As soon as his dad saw him, he waved and grinned, hurrying towards Andrew with Mum just behind.

'Look at you,' said Dad, taking Andrew's carrier bag from him. 'It didn't look like you at first, son. I'll go and get your bags from the driver.' He wandered off to the back of the coach while Andrew's mum hugged him embarrassingly.

'We'd better get you home for some tea, young man,' she said as his dad returned. 'Why don't you go and say thank you to your teachers before we leave?'

Andrew dutifully, but happily, went to thank all the staff in turn, all of whom seemed pleased that he'd done so. As he rejoined his parents by the gate, Andrew remembered the bird that he'd seen earlier.

'Do you know where the bird book is that Grandad bought me for Christmas last year, Mum?' he asked earnestly.

'I didn't think you were interested in all that sort of thing,' she answered, looking puzzled.

He smiled to himself, feeling suddenly full of emotion, before saying thoughtfully, 'A lot can change in a week.'

MENTAL SWITCH-ON

What makes home special? What do you most miss about home when you go away? What's difficult about coming home if you've had a good time while you've been away?

SO WHAT?

- Why might Andrew have been cautious about sitting with Jon?
- Why was the view more interesting to the boys on the way home than it had been on the way to the farm?
- Why didn't Mrs Denly just correct Andrew when he got the answer to her question wrong?
- How do you know when you're nearly home?
- Why do you think Andrew's dad had trouble recognising him?

PRAYER

Thank you for our homes,
for somewhere to feel safe and warm and dry,
and for somewhere to come back to when we've been away.
Amen

Index of curriculum and biblical links

NB: Further explanation and detail may be found after the table.

Chapter	Theme	Suggested Bible passages	PSHE links
1. I can't wait	Going on a journey	Genesis 12:1–9 (Abram); Exodus 1—16; Numbers 10:11–36 (Moses)	1a, 1b, 2e
2. You don't get out of it that easily	Promises	Genesis 15:1–21 (God's covenant with Abram); Mark 14:22–25 (Jesus' last meal with his friends)	1a, 1b, 2c, 2e, 4a. 4c, 4d
3. Follow the rules and you'll be fine	The importance of rules	Deuteronomy 5:1–22 (The Ten Commandments); Mark 12:28–34 (Jesus' great commandment)	1a, 1b, 2b, 2e, 3e

4. Sometimes it's good to give something up	Self-sacrifice	Genesis 22:1–19 (Abram and Isaac)	1a, 1b, 2e, 4a, 4c
5. Next time, think about it first, please	Consequences	Exodus 32:1–14 (Moses persuades God); Psalm 103:8–10 (God's mercy and love)	1a, 1b, 2c, 2e, 3f, 4a, 4c, 4d
6. Pass the salt, please, mate	Working and eating together	Luke 19:1–10 (Jesus and Zacchaeus); Luke 24:13–35 (Jesus breaks bread)	1a, 1b, 2e, 2i, 4a, 4b, 4c, 4d, 4e, 4f
7. Never be afraid to say you don't know	Humility	Matthew 5:5 (Jesus teaches about humility)	1a, 2e
8. Sorry, but it was me	Taking the blame	Romans 3:21–26 (How God puts us right with him)	1a, 2e, 2i, 4a, 4c, 4e, 4f
9. Life's too short to hold grudges	Forgiveness	Matthew 18:21–35 (Jesus teaches about forgiveness)	1a, 2c, 2e, 4a, 4c, 4d
10. It's just something someone gave me	Transformation	Galatians 5:16–26 (The Spirit and human nature)	1a, 2e, 3f, 4a, 4c
11. I try to be helpful	Peacemaking	Matthew 5:9 (Jesus teaches about peacemakers)	1a, 2c, 2e, 4a, 4c, 4d

12. You never see anything like this at home	Light and darkness	Genesis 1:1–5 (Creation); John 1:1–5; 8:12 (The light for the world)	1a, 2e
13. I can't believe how quick you've been	Living simply	Luke 18:18–30 (The rich man); Matthew 6:24–34 (Jesus teaches about possessions)	1a, 2e
14. I haven't felt this good in ages	Perseverance	Hebrews 12:1 (Running the race of life)	1a, 2e, 4a, 4c
15. I thought you'd nicked it	Being merciful	Matthew 5:7 (Jesus teaches about mercy)	1a, 2e, 2i, 4a, 4b, 4c
16. It can be amazing, too	Life and death	Ecclesiastes 3:1–8 (A time for everything)	1a, 2e 4c
17. It was nothing	Freedom	Luke 4:16–21 (Jesus teaches in Nazareth)	1a, 2e, 3e, 3f, 4a, 4c
18. I'm good, thanks	Possibilities	Genesis 37:5–11 (Joseph and his dreams)	1a, 2e, 4a, 4c
19. I've got everything I want in here	Family life	1 Corinthians 13:4–8 (Paul teaches about love)	1a, 2e, 4a, 4c

| 20. A lot can change in a week | Homecoming | Psalm 122 (In praise of Jerusalem); Psalm 137:4–6 (Taken away from home); Luke 15:11–32 (The lost son) | 1a, 2e, 4c |

DETAILED REFERENCES

This collection of stories visits the following general themes and ideas from the latest non-statutory guidance for PSHE and RE at KS2. Unfortunately, detailed RE curriculum references are not currently available, as the responsibility for devising the RE curriculum lies with an Agreed Syllabus Conference (ASC) established by each Local Authority's Standing Advisory Council on Religious Education (SACRE). At the time of writing, the government has halted the development of a national set of curriculum guidelines for Primary RE, a situation which may change in time. However, I have included summary statements for the RE curriculum taken from the most recent non-statutory guidance, published early in 2010. Up-to-date information should be available for PSHE on the Department for Education website, and for RE on the Religious Education Council of England and Wales website.

PSHE

Developing confidence and responsibility and making the most of their abilities.

1. Pupils should be taught:
   a. to talk and write about their opinions, and explain their views, on issues that affect themselves and society;

b. to recognise their worth as individuals by identifying positive things about themselves and their achievements, seeing their mistakes, making amends and setting personal goals.

Preparing to play an active role as citizens

2. Pupils should be taught:
    a. why and how rules and laws are made and enforced, why different rules are needed in different situations and how to take part in making and changing rules;
    b. to realise the consequences of anti-social and aggressive behaviours, such as bullying and racism, on individuals and communities;
    c. that there are different kinds of responsibilities, rights and duties at home, at school and in the community, and that these can sometimes conflict with each other;
    d. to reflect on spiritual, moral, social and cultural issues, using imagination to understand other people's experiences;
    e. to appreciate the range of national, regional, religious and ethnic identities in the United Kingdom.

Developing a healthy, safer lifestyle

3. Pupils should be taught:
    a. to recognise the different risks in different situations and then decide how to behave responsibly, including sensible road use, and judging what kind of physical contact is acceptable or unacceptable;
    b. that pressure to behave in an unacceptable or risky way can come from a variety of sources, including people they know, and how to ask for help and use basic techniques for resisting pressure to do wrong.

Developing good relationships and respecting the differences between people

4. Pupils should be taught:
   a. that their actions affect themselves and others, to care about other people's feelings and to try to see things from their points of view;
   b. to think about the lives of people living in other places and times, and people with different values and customs;
   c. to be aware of different types of relationship, including marriage and those between friends and families, and to develop the skills to be effective in relationships;
   d. to realise the nature and consequences of racism, teasing, bullying and aggressive behaviours, and how to respond to them and ask for help;
   e. to recognise and challenge stereotypes;
   f. that differences and similarities between people arise from a number of factors, including cultural, ethnic, racial and religious diversity, gender and disability.

RE

In summary, religious education for children and young people:

- Provokes challenging questions about the meaning and purpose of life, beliefs, the self, issues of right and wrong, and what it means to be human. It develops pupils' knowledge and understanding of Christianity, other principal religions, and religious traditions that examine these questions, fostering personal reflection and spiritual development.
- Encourages pupils to explore their own beliefs (whether they are religious or non-religious), in the light of what they learn, as they examine issues of religious belief and faith and how these impact on personal, institutional and social ethics; and

to express their responses. This also builds resilience to anti-democratic or extremist narratives.
- Enables pupils to build their sense of identity and belonging, which helps them flourish within their communities and as citizens in a diverse society.
- Teaches pupils to develop respect for others, including people with different faiths and beliefs, and helps to challenge prejudice.
- Prompts pupils to consider their responsibilities to themselves and to others, and to explore how they might contribute to their communities and to wider society. It encourages empathy, generosity and compassion.

RE has an important part to play as part of a broad, balanced and coherent curriculum to which all pupils are entitled. High-quality learning experiences in RE are designed and provided by careful planning through locally agreed syllabuses and in schools, taking into account the need to offer breadth of content, depth of learning and coherence between concepts, skills and content.

BIBLICAL REFERENCES

Just one or two suggestions have been included of examples of each of the themes or ideas on which each story is based. Since 'central Judeo-Christian truths' (as they are termed in the Introduction) have been chosen, there are inevitably many more references available, and teachers may find more appropriate ones than those mentioned.